To Maria
thank you
for walking w.
in the Halls of knw.

one
white
crow

Brenda

George McMullen

author of *Red Snake*

With the Research Papers of J.N. Emerson, Ph.D.
on Psychic Archaeology

Foreword by
Raymond W. Worring

Introduction by
Stephan A. Schwartz

one
white
crow

HAMPTONROADS
PUBLISHING COMPANY, INC.

For information write:

Hampton Roads Publishing Company, Inc.
891 Norfolk Square
Norfolk, VA 23502

Or call: (804)459-2453
FAX: (804)455-8907

If you are unable to order this book from your local
bookseller, you may order directly from the publisher.
Quantity discounts for organizations are available.
Call 1-800-766-8009, toll-free.

ISBN 1-57174-007-4

Printed on acid-free paper in the United States of America

*This book
is dedicated to
the memory of
Dr. J. Norman Emerson
my friend.*

*My thanks to
Ann Emerson
and my wife
Charlotte
who made it all possible.*

J.N. Emerson, Ph.D.
1914-1978

Dr. Emerson, Professor Emeritus of Anthropology, University of Toronto, was widely known and respected as a teacher and for his archaeological work with the Hurons, the Ontario Iroquois.

He was, in his own words, "a stones and bones" archaeologist for 30 years, until his association with me demonstrated that there were other, less traditional means of obtaining provable information about man's prehistory.

The pages that follow chronicle the events that marked his foray into this unknown territory seldom explored by academics.

Red Snake, one of the unseen Guides in this search, says:

Many people walk
this earth.
Few leave footprints
to follow.

J.N. Emerson did.

Ann Emerson's Comments

The publication of this book brings me satisfaction. I was, as is told herein, closely associated with my husband's work from its inception and participated in all the many changes and growing pains involved in the research as it progressed, as well as most of the travel incidental to it.

It was I who brought George McMullen and Professor Emerson together and found most of the other psychics whom he briefly used in his exploration into these mystical realms which helped him in beginning to understand how to effectively use George's extraordinary abilities.

Since I am trained as an editor, I feel I also helped to bring clarity and authenticity to what my husband wrote and have, I believe, helped to do the same for this book. Many of the articles and reports that have been published on this fascinating research have had troubling errors of fact or of interpretation in them.

George McMullen and his wonderful wife Charlotte have now been my personal friends for more than 20 years. They have been of inestimable help and support to me in my personal life, as they were to Norman in his research; and of course they were his friends, as well. I am grateful to George for bringing my late husband's work together in such a readable and accurate way. I hope that those who read this book will find inspiration from it, as we who have known it as it unfolded have.

Ann Emerson
1993

Table of Contents

Foreword

"The whole history of scientific advancement is full of scientists investigating phenomena the Establishment did not believe were there."

—Margaret Mead

For many years the staff of the Investigative Research Field Station and I have been intimately involved with law enforcement in the capacity of developing and implementing special crime-control programs. During this period of time we concentrated our efforts on innovative investigative techniques. One of the techniques explored was the use of intuitives in criminal investigations. A great deal of time and effort went into identifying and recruiting potential intuitives or psychics, testing their abilities, developing techniques of psychic investigation, following up leads obtained, and evaluating their effectiveness as an investigative adjunct. We were sufficiently impressed with our experiences to encourage the future use of psychic ability in criminal investigations and to publish a book, *Psychic Criminology*, which is a comprehensive operations manual for using psychics as an investigative adjunct and is applicable to any field of inquiry. We found that when properly recruited, tested, and utilized professionally, psychics have proven to be of substantial value to the investigator. It was during this research period that we met and worked with George McMullen. George had already established an impressive track record for using his intuitive abilities in the service of archaeology while working with Dr. Norman Emerson.

One of the most interesting psychic skills, especially to an investigator, is the ability to psychometrize. Psychometry is the extrasensory perception of the history of an object, including the people and events connected with it, usually through handling the object. Psychometry often seems to be a form of "retrocognition," which is the ability to experience past events which are not in the memory of the individual undergoing the experience. The object held becomes the key or vehicle to the past event or experience. Criminologically, this ability is used to *help reconstruct a crime* through the psychic handling of items of physical evidence or visiting the crime scene itself. This is the essence of criminal investigation in its search for the truth—to reconstruct the crime scene. Similarly, the essence of archaeology is to reconstruct the archaeological site. To this end, proven psychics can be of inestimable value as the excellent papers in this book demonstrate.

The time is ripe for a systematic and professional use of psychics by archaeologists. It must be remembered that even the best investigators have failures; they don't solve every crime. The same is true with psychically-assisted archaeological research. Yet to discount its use and to deny its possibilities is short-sighted and unrealistic in the face of the overwhelming evidence in favor of its use. As Dr. Emerson's papers show, the proper use of psychics can be a valuable tool in site location and cultural reconstruction.

However, its acceptance as a research tool is a challenge. To get some idea of the extent of this challenge, one has only to review the history of scientific discoveries. Each new idea or discovery has been met with hostility and prejudices from the established order. The discoverers have been insulted, assaulted, and even imprisoned. Careers have been ruined and, even worse, important breakthroughs have been delayed for decades. As Freud observed, our relationship with science must be paradoxical because we are forced to pay an almost intolerable price for each major gain in knowledge. Yet nothing seems to be able to stop an idea whose time has come. "Intuition in the service of research" is an idea whose time has come. And credit is due to Dr. Emerson and his psychic informant, George McMullen, for being willing to risk personal reputation and even career to pioneer an exciting and important new field and methodology of inquiry.

Raymond W. Worring, Director
Investigative Research Field Station

Preface: Archaeology and Mysticism
From Dr. Emerson's Papers

[The following was found in Dr. Emerson's papers and shows that he had intended to write a book on his research during his lifetime, but unfortunately he was not able to do so. I felt that it would be proper to include his preface in this book.]

Archaeology and Mysticism

This is a book about what to me were "mind-boggling" experiences. These were generated by a combination of archaeological and psychic studies. It began as fun and games, but as time passed it became serious, exciting, and meaningful study.

I do not yet present my studies as being "scientific." Nor are they fully understood or "proven." Yet my purpose has been to pursue and seek to understand the phenomena observed as rigorously, skeptically, and scientifically as possible. As time passed and my study progressed, my skepticism has been tempered by recognizing the need to have a measure of faith and belief in my work. My views upon the nature of science have had to undergo changes and redefinition. I have sought always to remain objective and rigorous in dealing with the phenomena recorded and studied.

Although I do not claim that my studies have achieved the status of being scientific, neither can they be ignored or dismissed as nonsense, imagination, or hallucinations. The key to the matter appears to lie in the concept of *intuition*. I found for my purpose a workable definition of *intuition* is that individuals exist who have "an immediate knowledge or knowing of events without the obvious use of learning or reason."

My own area of expertise is archaeology (the investigation and recovery of man's prehistory). Intuitive or psychic individuals can tell me about past events and circumstances by a poorly-understood process of "immediate knowing." My role in this study has been to use my background of learned knowledge to assess the accuracy or the degree of truth contained in the statements they have given me.

It rapidly became evident that by availing myself of such sources of information—using intuitive or psychic informants—a whole new picture of man's past was readily available. Moreover, the story of prehistory so revealed was richer, deeper, more human,and—in the last analysis—perhaps more "true" than the story of man's past that has been produced by the writings of traditional scientific archaeologists to date, with almost no exception.

Yet matters are not quite so simple as that sounds; the intuitive readings were not always correct. In fact, there were some cases which had to be judged absolutely wrong; and there were many cases where I did not have the knowledge or ability to judge.

Over a period of years I have formulated a sort of rule-of-thumb approach to the readings of psychic informants: capable informants are about 80 to 90 percent correct. As for the individual psychic reading, about one-third of the statements have been almost immediately recognizable as on target, verifiable, accurate, and so presumably "true."

A second third of the material is not immediately recognizable but can be verified and validated by further research. The final third is of such a nature as to be not verifiable by any known means. I must confess that, having gone through the process many times, I consider it important to also pay close attention to this last third of seemingly unverifiable information.

In working with my psychic informants, I have tried very hard to maintain a sound perspective and a sense of balance. I have sought to keep to the subjects in which I am trained—archaeology and anthropology—but it has not been easy. It is inevitable that one comes to realize that psychics who can provide intuitive knowledge of the past can also know and produce knowledge of both the present and sometimes even the future that are equally mind-boggling. In many ways, help and guidance with the questions "Who am I?" "What am I?" "What will I be?" or "What is in store for me?" are questions that plague and interest all human beings. Information like this leads one to question even the nature of time itself.

Such questions are beyond my scope of study because they do

not permit testing and verification and so bring about reasonable assessment in the way that the study of man's past can. Going down such byways was, I found, a diversion that had to be excluded. What others sought to have my informants find out for them—no matter how personally urgent it might be for them—did not lead to fruitful use of time and energies available for the research.

From the very onset of my work, I attempted to treat intuition as one of many ways of obtaining knowledge about the past. As I continued to work with psychics, I sought to understand the information process further. This search led me to consider many levels of psychic information-producing phenomena such as the Ouija board, tarot cards, the pendulum, tea cup reading, crystal ball gazing, and a variety of methods of psychometry.

I gradually gained knowledge of what I would call "high levels" of psychic performance induced by such methods as hypnotism, sensory deprivation, semi-trance, and deep-trance mediumship. There was an impressive sameness and overlapping of such phenomena, and, probably because of my anthropological background, I sought to take part in, to observe, and to record such experiences. I was not an active participant, but as much as possible a neutral observer in these sessions.

I have undergone many experiences that have contributed to my understanding, development, and, I believe, enlightenment. This has called for a constantly open—but not uncritical—mind, and it does call for a sense of humour. Otherwise, the usually predictable, orderly world would become unbalanced and quite impossible. Impossible events have become not the exception but more the rule in my current life.

I finally became aware of ingredients in my pursuit of understanding that can only be described inadequately as "spiritual." I began to realize that unknown forces had to be involved; that in some way my research was being "led." I was struck by "meaningful coincidences" that were far beyond chance possibilities.

I also had to learn to believe in and to have faith in the successful outcome of my studies and to constantly work to maintain a high motivation: that is, we were to address our program to matters of good that were of future concern to humanity.

I can only ask the reader to accept that what I write is done in all honesty; that what is recorded actually happened, however unusual or unexplainable.

There are hundreds of hours of taped information for scrutiny— far beyond what is contained in this book. I have pursued this study for untold hours, months, and years because I want it to become part and parcel of everyday knowledge.

I believe that the experiences I have been privileged to have are but a small part of what is available to humanity. I hope there are significant signs of a snowballing revolution or evolution of the increased spiritual nature and awareness of human beings that is everywhere evident to those who will but look at it with an open mind. This should have great impact on the future of mankind at a time when we so evidently require change in positive directions.

It is for this reason that again I note that what started out almost a curious game in seeking to relate archaeology to psychic studies gradually turned into something much more serious and fulfilling than I had expected. I would be the first to state that it has had a great impact upon my own life and I welcome the reader to consider and to share this.

I invite you to join me in a novel and exciting journey, "to walk in my moccasins" back into the past with the help of my psychic studies as we attempt to better understand the "true" meaning of human prehistory and man's past, judged against our current knowledge of archaeology. Perhaps in the process we may further understand and learn of man's spirituality and potential for future development.

It has long been a rationalization of the discipline of archaeology that for man to cope with his unknown future he will be better equipped if he has detailed understanding of his own past. I propose to use an innovative approach to this understanding by combining the disciplines of archaeology, science, and psychic studies.

Introduction

This small volume is a book to be read at two levels. At one it is an historical document, opening a window onto a landscape where psi and science meet. It records the work of Professor Norman Emerson, one of Canada's pre-eminent archaeologists, indeed, considered by many to be the "father of scientific archaeology in Canada," who came to intuitive methodologies late in his career. This late timing was a happy eventuality, however, since by then Emerson had accumulated the kudos and awards that a rigidly mainstream career of excellence draws to itself and, from that bully pulpit, he got a hearing for psychic archaeology that a lesser name could never have obtained. At the second level, the book is a memorabilia to a friendship, one of those felicitous happenings which bring change in science, even as they nurture the participants. Norman Emerson and his psychic informant, George McMullen, might seem an unlikely pair: the one learned in his field and academic in his manner, the other blue-collar in his background and bluff working man in his style. But those were superficials only. As Emerson said, ". . .we were thrown together and our association developed along the average lines of Canadian males of our age and station in life. That is, we had cars, trucks, boats, fishing gear, and a few dollars in the banks at the end of each month. We both had three children and shared a love of the great outdoors and times of relative silence." Clearly, they held in common the things that count.

They did something else for one another. They each validated a part of the other's core personality; a part which, until their friendship, had been denied. From my conversations with each of them I know that this exchange was a highly meaningful gift.

For McMullen, Emerson provided the imprimatur of science. It was something for which McMullen had, not surprisingly, hungered all his life. It is not hard to see why. To grow up and protect and keep his psychic ability functioning was no small feat. I have often wondered whether I could have grown up half so well with a talent my friends and family not only did not recognize but, to a painful degree, despised. Emerson was a careful man, and he did careful things. As he points out, "archaeology attracts. . .systematic people. . ." He was an exemplar of the type and his meticulousness gave definition and validation for McMullen's words which meant a great deal.

The exchange went both ways. To Emerson, McMullen gave a way to explore a part of himself that he had never acknowledged. Every archaeologist with whom I have ever spoken has told me that at certain times, and in certain places, there was a sure knowingness as to where a site was located or where something would be found. But most would resist the idea that the psychic played any role in their choices. When challenged, each would say something like, "It's true, I couldn't explain it just as reasoning. Maybe it was luck. But still. . ." And, then, uncomfortable with where the conversation was heading, they would change its tack. The fact is, however, that after one sifts out the vision of an eye made expert over many digs and a mind filled with the literature of the craft, there still remains an irreducible portion that intellect and insight cannot explain, and the hand-waving of luck will not make plausible. In the end, one is left with the archaeologist's own unacknowledged psychic functioning. McMullen showed Emerson, in clear terms, and by "the test of the spade," archaeology's hallowed benchmark, the reality of psychic information. McMullen's very lack of formal education became a strength for Emerson. His accurate though sometimes quaint layman's words—maulers for teeth—in a field filled with terms of art became proof of integrity. His location of things which could be found in no other manner forced a re-evaluation of Emerson's world view. McMullen's psychic insights also affected the most fundamental issue a middle-aged man faces, his physical health. With adherence to McMullen's insights, Emerson, by his own admission, "bought several years of life."

And so these two men, supporting one another in the working world of Canadian males, and drawing out from one another the resolution of long-dormant portions of their own beings, began an adventure in tandem that has affected many lives, my own included. The tales of these forays are described within this book, in the extracts from papers presented as scientific conferences, and in the unpublished journals and reminiscences each recorded.

For me the most impressive and scientifically significant of all these accounts lies in the story of the Boyes site, an Iroquois village dig carried out by C.S. Reid, a graduate student of Emerson's, then working on his masters at McMasters University. It would become the first graduate degree in archaeology ever given by a department of recognized stature for work in which the psychic played an overt role.

Paddy Reid had worked his site so long we can say with some confidence that if intellect were the font of answers, there would already have been answers aplenty. There were none. Indeed, it was Reid's desperation, sweetened, I am sure, by his respect for his former professor, that led him to try the course McMullen offered. If he had had other options he would surely have been less attentive to what McMullen proposed, particularly since, to both Reid and Emerson, much of what McMullen said seemed almost embarrassingly wrong. Most striking of all was his placement of the village palisade and the entry way he described. I will not steal the thunder of the story, but I draw it to the reader's particular attention.

What made Boyes so significant? The answer in fullness would be longer than an introduction could be decently stretched; but there are certain headlines. In any project in which psychic information plays a role, the question which must be asked is: "Could the respondent know these things through intellectual sources, or through normal sensory input?" Put another way, what is the *a priori* probability of the psychic observations? If one is looking for a ship, general statements about hulls are pretty meaningless. Observations that the captain's great cabin has a crystal chandelier are not. Such a thing would be well outside the expected, and making such a comment seemingly a flight of fancy. Should it prove correct, it must be given a special weight. The beauty of the Boyes site is that so many of McMullen's observations had just such a low probability, could not be explained as intellectual analysis, or careful observation, and yet proved to be so uncannily accurate.

Finally, underlying the narrative in these episodes one should be aware of Emerson's struggle to develop ways of testing the accuracy of psychic information which was not amenable to the test of the spade yet was still important, and to realize how much of what a psychic respondent like McMullen says can never be tested. How can we know in any absolute way what lies in the heart of an Iroquois warrior? We can know what we might feel in similar circumstances, *but not what was actually felt*, absent a journal entry by the person sensible to the feelings themselves. I point this out because, when looked at objectively, it is obvious that the challenges attendant to marrying the psychic with science lie as much with the inadequacies of the latter as the former. Emerson says repeatedly that he found McMullen's information "to be about 80 percent correct." Over 17 years of experiments, evaluated by independent third-party experts, and with a strong emphasis on information—including a great deal proffered by McMullen himself—which has a low *a priori* probability that can tested by excavation, I would place the mark closer to 75 percent; but that, at this stage of our understanding, is but a quibble over something that is by definition extraordinary. Our real challenge at this juncture is to learn how to predict prior to excavation which psychic statements will comprise the 75 or 80 percent, and which the 20 to 25. As strange as it may seem to a world conditioned to honor only the analytical, the obstacle to that solution lies not with the psychic but with the scientific. Emerson puts a figure on McMullen's accuracy, but not on archaeology's. He does not say what all archaeologists know to be true. Even when their science is at its best, its accuracy is very partial, and much that is discovered can not be understood at all. Typically, it has been my experience that no more than 50 percent of the information we give over to independent specialists can be evaluated at all. As to archaeology's ability to locate sites in the first place, even the most ardent supporter would accept that finds result more from serendipity than otherwise.

The fact that after carrying out over a dozen psychic archaeological experiments around the world, including a comparison of electronic remote sensing—sonars, magnetometers, satellite images and the like—with intuitive remote sensing, both evaluated by independent third parties, I believe that if I could have only one method of finding an archaeological site I would choose the psychic above all others. It will discomfort many, I know, but science goes, or at least should go, where evidence—not prejudice—leads. Norman Emerson and George McMullen have blazed a trail worthy of being followed.

Stephan A. Schwartz
Los Angeles, California
September 1993

Chapter 1

Dr. Norman Emerson and George McMullen: Who We Are and How We Met

Legend has it that there is no such thing as a White Crow. I believe there is. I am one who has been compared to a White Crow, because I am not like most other people. I am a psychic; I psychometrize objects. That is to say, I hold an artifact in my hand and information comes to me as to who made it, where it was made, and the time it was made—often in the far past. I get this information without studying or reading. It just comes to me, though it does take concentration and focus.

I met Dr. J. Norman Emerson in 1969. My wife Charlotte and his wife Ann were friends, and it was inevitable that we should meet sometime. I had been told he was an archaeologist but had paid scant attention to this. I thought he was going to be the usual academic type—aloof and a bit stuffy. I was therefore pleasantly surprised to find a very friendly man who was not at all as I expected. We became friends immediately. This was not usual, as you would wonder what an educated man would find in common with a man without an academic education.

Norm kept his big words for his peers and never used them on me. He was a mature person in his fifties when I met him. He was bald with a fringe of curly grey hair. His eyes had a perpetual twinkle and he had a ready laugh. His sense of humour was subtle but never insulting. He never talked down to anyone and felt deeply for his fellow man. He was always active and had a great zest for life. Never in the time I knew him did he ever say anything bad about anyone—even those he didn't like, and these were few indeed. By the time we met he had reached a zenith in his profession. He was liked and respected by his colleagues and students.

After we had known each other for a while, Ann mentioned to him that I could psychometrize objects. He decided to try me out on some artifacts as described in the following pages. I did not want this to be publicized at the time. I was still a little afraid of being ridiculed and preferred not to subject my family to questions from relatives and friends. But I had never before dealt with a man the calibre of Norman Emerson.

John Norman Emerson, Ph.D., was a full professor of anthropology and Director of Archaeological Studies at the University of Toronto where he had taught, in his own words, "stones and bones" archaeology for more than 25 years. He was the co-founding vice president and later president of the Canadian Archaeological Association.

Norman's field of specialty was the Ontario Iroquois (Huron), but he had also spent two summers excavating in the Canadian Arctic and had dug in Illinois and Wisconsin while doing work on his doctorate at the University of Chicago. He was one of the first three archaeologists in Canada and was known as the Dean of Canadian Archaeologists. At one point it was noted that 90 percent of those working as professionals in archaeology in Canada had started their work under his tutelage.

But perhaps it would be better to quote Dr. Emerson's own words as to how we met. Going through his papers I found the following paragraphs that he had written, presumably the beginning of a book he was considering writing. I quote:

How did George and I meet? What is he like? Is it true that he is part Indian? What does George work at? These are typical questions I have been asked about George. They probably merit answers because they are all part of our developing and continuing relationship.

I can offer many reasons why George and I met: I could say it was rather mystical—that we had shared former lifetimes together and that we were simply taking up where we left off—and leave it at that, or I could say that our wives met, and so we met, and leave it at that. It is quite possible that neither explanation is entirely satisfactory.

Why did my wife and George's wife meet? Well, at that time George lived in Markham and we lived at Bond Lake, near Oak Ridges, Ontario. My wife and George's wife, as is so common these days, became members of a study group dedicated to self-development, awareness, and that sort of thing. They shared a mutual interest in the readings of that great prophet and psychic, Edgar Cayce. Neither George nor I shared our wives' interest in these matters, except to admit it was probably a good thing and that they were having "fun," a sort of husbandly tolerance.

However, the explanation can be more complicated than that when you look at the statistical odds, as parapsychologists and, for that matter, others must. How did Edgar Cayce come into the picture and with it a continuing investment on my wife's part in the whole broad field of psychic studies? She is much more widely read and informed upon such matters than I am, and is thus an inestimable source of help in my work as it proceeds. Within limits I am generally several jumps behind her reading.

Whatever the case was, I did not share that interest and did not attend the meetings. These studies became a consuming interest in my wife's life, and so as a result she met George's wife Charlotte, and eventually I met George. Simple coincidence, or preordained? Who knows? It will soon become evident that the reader of this text will be well-advised to maintain a source of perspective about the underlying ordering of events in evaluating the material presented.

At the time, I was making only a moderately successful attempt to combat a problem of alcoholism which was of great concern to my wife and of rather less concern to me. I was not exactly in good shape.

Now, back in 1970, my wife was concerned about my health and also a believer in a combination of good nutrition and psychic healing to take care of health problems. The net result was that she sought out George to do a psychic reading for me.

The general tenor of the message was that my health was in serious trouble and I had better shape up or there were going to be serious consequences. Ann came home and told me about this, but not who the psychic was.

It was my first knowledge of this kind of ability and the real caring and concern expressed for my well-being. I did not make a big noise about it, but I heeded the advice.

Ann and Charlotte decided that their husbands should meet man to man without my knowledge that George was the one who had done the reading, and so we were introduced. Our lives were not unduly unusual and gradually material interests developed. As Charlotte and Ann became best friends, we were thrown together and our association developed along the average lines of Canadian males of our age and station in life. That is, we had cars, trucks, boats, fishing gear, and a few dollars in the bank at the end of the month. We both had three children and shared a love of the great outdoors and times of relative silence.

As events transpired, we did intervisiting in our home at Bond Lake and at George's fine summer cottage in the Kawartha Lakes district. Such events were largely party times with boating, fishing, beer drinking, singsongs, and card playing becoming major parts of the activity. Psychic matters and archaeology were generally far from our minds. This situation continued for a considerable time.

Celebrations such as New Year's Eve parties became integrated into the picture as George and his family moved from Markham to Peterborough, Ontario. By this time I had learned that George was the psychic who had read for me about my health. So it came about that on January 1, 1971, I gave George artifacts and he held them and "read" them for me in his kitchen while Ann took notes on what he said. The reading was so fascinating and accurate that I knew at once that this sort of research was something I wanted to pursue. And so it all began—my work in what I call *intuitive archaeology.*

When Dr. Emerson gave his first paper on intuitive archaeology, I was in the audience listening to his speech. Archaeology at that time was just beginning to be accepted as a science by the academic community, and what Dr. Emerson was about to say sent shock waves through the people with whom he worked. Here was a man who had spent more than 30 years building up an enviable reputation among his associates and he was this day risking his credibility among them.

It was after this meeting and Norm's willingness to risk all that I decided to come out of the closet, so to speak. That day Dr. J.N. Emerson proved what a brilliant scientist he was. It proved beyond a doubt that he had the courage to speak up and to look at other than accepted and conventional means to advance man's knowledge of past events in human progress.

On the following pages I am going to quote directly from papers Dr. Emerson presented to various meetings over the next three years and from writings that were found among his papers concerning our work together and with other intuitive or psychic people. They are copied word-for-word from his original text.

Chapter 2

Dr. Emerson Speaks About His First Paper on His Experience With Psychic Phenomena

[Among Dr. Emerson's papers was the following about how the first public statement he made came to be given and about his feelings in giving it.]

Those who attended Session VII, entitled "Methodology," at the annual meeting of the Canadian Archaeological Association at Simon Fraser University, Burnaby, British Columbia, on Friday afternoon, March 26, 1973, probably had little comprehension of what they were to hear; all they had to go on was the abstract outlined below:

> Intuition has been described as "the immediate learning or knowing of something without the conscious use of reasoning." In actual fact, the whole research program defies reason and the usual concept of the rational man. The ultimate implications of this alliance of archaeology and parapsychology are, to say the least, mind-boggling.

The use of the term *mind-boggling* in retrospect may well appear a strange choice; but at the time it was submitted for inclusion in the program, that was the way I felt about the matter. Time has not changed my attitude.

My paper was the last on the list for Friday afternoon, preceded by scholarly papers dealing with problems of data processing and of clustering and scaling a site series and the difficulties of making descriptive types scientifically honourable. The stress and impact of science was self-evident. My friend George and I seemed to stand somewhat naked in the Computer Age.

But there we were at the end of the program. It did me good

to see him, his wife, and my wife sitting far up in the gallery—George smiling confidently, surrounded by his anonymity, which he was later to break at the reception and annual banquet the next night.

I will go on record as saying, for the information of those who were not aware of it, that I was extremely nervous when I began my presentation. For one who has the years of lecturing experience that I have had, this case of nerves had to be significant and unusual. Yet such was the case.

At the time I was extremely grateful to a tiny little baby whose mother had brought it to the lecture. In an atmosphere of considerable silence as I began to talk, the baby, who chose not to protect its anonymity, began to cry. I found those little cries most relaxing. They broke my tension and I was able to proceed with minimal difficulty. I will always be grateful to that tiny child.

Besides being nervous, I was also physically ill that day. When I woke up in the morning, I had a splitting headache. My appetite was nonexistent. I just lay in bed and didn't get up until early afternoon. The last time I recall being this ill was one Friday, years ago, when I received a telegram from the University of Chicago, instructing me that I would defend my doctoral thesis the following Monday morning at noon. It was, perhaps—at least to me—a similar crisis period in my life.

My nervousness was further increased by the fact that George was rather late in picking me up to drive me to the university. At that point it did not help when I slammed the car door on the tail of George's good old dog, Royal. The justified howls and hurt eyes of Royal did little to calm my nerves. It was with this background that I walked into the lecture room to deliver my talk and to learn, moreover, that it was scheduled to be given half an hour earlier than I had expected, since a previous speaker had not arrived.

In some mysterious way the cry of that tiny baby relieved my tension and kindled my sense of humour and perhaps that of the waiting audience. My talk was delivered.

Chapter 3

Intuitive Archaeology:
A Psychic Approach
A Paper by Dr. Emerson

[This, Dr. Emerson's first paper about intuitive archaeology, was presented to The Canadian Archaeological Association in March 1973.]

Intuition can be usefully defined as "the immediate knowing or learning of something without the conscious use of reasoning." It is my conviction that I have received knowledge about archaeology, artifacts, and archaeological sites from a psychic informant who relates this information without any evidence of the conscious use of reasoning.

My psychic informant, who at the present time wishes to remain anonymous, is named George. I presented George with a fragment of an artifact from the Black Creek site located in metropolitan Toronto. He held the fragment in his hand, contemplated it, fondled it, and meditated on it at length. He then correctly told me it was a pipe stem, told me the age of the site it came from, and told me the location of the site. He described how the pipe was manufactured, described the maker, and provided details about the community and living conditions. He then took pencil and paper in hand and drew a picture of the pipe bowl, which he stated belonged to the broken pipe stem.

Figure 1. Artifact psychometrically studied by George McMullen.

*Figure 2. Drawing traced from the original done by
George McMullen as he perceived it psychometrically.*

I was fascinated and impressed because I immediately recognized
that he had clearly drawn a picture of a typical Iroquois conical
ring bowl pipe. This type of pipe was one of the popular types
recovered from the Black Creek site and is one of the predominate
types to be found in middle Iroquois times. I next gave George a
fragmented human effigy pipe bowl recovered from the shore of
Bass Lake near Orillia, Ontario. George again provided me with
a wealth of information about this artifact related to its age and
function and details about its general setting and location. Once
again, he took pencil and paper and drew a picture of the modeled
human effigy head which he stated had been broken off the edge
of the pipe bowl.

Again, fascinated and impressed, I recognized the drawing as
that of a typical Huron pinch-faced human effigy. This pipe is
characteristic of late prehistoric sites in the Simcoe County area.

To present this case, I have sought answers to five complex
questions.

1. Has George gained this knowledge by study?

2. If not, does George read my mind?

3. If not, does George receive information by mental
telepathy?

4. Is George always correct in his statements?

5. Can his statements be verified?

1. To answer question one: Has George gained this knowledge by study? The answer is definitely No.

George has a minimum of formal education. During the Great Depression, he left school to go to work. George is not an avid reader. He has done little reading about Indians and has been exposed to no in-depth reading about Ontario Iroquois.

He states that he visited the Royal Ontario Museum only once and was disturbed by the mummies.

George would concur in my statement that in the field of Iroquois prehistory he is both uneducated and uninformed. I stress that it is the very truth of this fact that gives both strength and evidence to the conclusions that his statements are intuitive—that is, they are the essence, the product of intuition—"immediate knowing without the conscious use of reasoning."

Incidently, by the use of the terms "uneducated" and "uninformed" I do not wish to convey the impression that George is an ignorant, tongue-tied, dull oaf. He is not. He is a warm, intelligent, and thoughtful human being. He is my friend. He is just not cluttered up and overlaid with pedantic and restrictive booklearning. His knowledge is definitely not the result of scholarly study.

It was experiences such as these which led me to pursue my studies with George and, as will become evident, of George. I have now been pursuing this research for two years and am convinced that George is providing me with information on Indian pre-history that is accurate about 80 percent of the time and that this knowledge is the product of George's intuition.

2. Does George read my mind? The answer to this question, I believe, is No. I hasten to add that if he were doing this and no more, it would be a phenomenon worthy of study and investigation.

George does tell me things that coincide with my own knowledge and thus he could be simply reading my mind; but he also makes statements of new knowledge and statements that disagree with my knowledge and expectations. These areas of new knowledge and disagreement suggest to me that George is doing much more than just reading my mind. I offer two examples. The first deals with new knowledge. In response to a newspaper article about George, a lady wrote to me that she had an old coin that she would like to know about, if possible. She mailed the coin to me from the town of Markstay. The location of this town was unknown to me, and I did not mention the name to George.

The coin was of the George III vintage and literally could have come from anywhere in the world. He clearly identified the finder and the loser of the coin. When I asked where it was found, he immediately said, "Sudbury, North Bay, Callander." The next day I checked the Atlas and Markstay was located 20 miles east of Sudbury and 60 miles west of North Bay and Callander. To me, this was an identification of great accuracy. George could not have learned this from me; and, of course, he did not mention Markstay, per se.

The next example involves an area of disagreement. George and I visited the prehistoric Iroquois Quackenbush village site, north of Peterborough, Ontario. Among other things, George told me that these people did not cultivate corn, beans, and squash. I found it hard to accept the idea that they did not have these traditional Iroquois crops. The investigating archaeologist assured me that they had recovered abundant evidence of corn, squash, and sunflower seeds. At this point it appeared that George was wrong. The thought then came to my mind: perhaps they had obtained their vegetables by trade from the south, rather than by local cultivation. George had stressed their trade in hides, and the investigating archaeologist felt he could make a good case for trade in stone.

I then had soil samples taken and studied for pollen grains, which remain indefinitely in the ground. This study revealed one problematic corn pollen grain. This did not seem to argue for local cultivation. This was especially suggested by the relative abundance of pollen evidence of various trees, plants, and grasses. At this point it would seem George was correct; however, I do not feel that the pollen studies have been extensive enough to be conclusive. They must be further expanded.

Thus, these examples involving new knowledge and disagreement will, I hope, serve to demonstrate that George is doing much more than reading my mind.

3. Is George receiving his information by some form of mental telepathy? Cases of mental telepathy are abundantly documented. George could be unconsciously receiving messages from the lady in Markstay, or from the Quackenbush investigating archaeologist. But in most cases of telepathy, the sender is named or otherwise identified or suggested. There was nothing of this kind in George's statements.

The strongest argument against mental telepathy of the more usual kind is the fact that the bulk of George's statements relate to a very dim and distant past. They relate to a period anywhere from five centuries to 6000 years ago. It almost seems as if he is receiving telepathic information from people who were there at the time and who had specific information about these times.

It is difficult to even begin to offer a comprehensive or even a comprehensible explanation of the above phenomena. They certainly involve more than traditional mental telepathy.

I have explanatory thoughts of my own, but at this point in my studies, it would seem more prudent to reserve judgment for the future. Much of the answers must ultimately lie in an understanding of George. Certain processes are clear to me; his statements are the crystallization of selected auditory and visual images available to him. One further fact about George must be noted: that is, his extreme sensitivity to the artifacts that he handles. He describes them as hot or cold, dead or alive.

This is apparently a temperature assessment. The colder, the older. The fact that his age assessments are quite accurate stands as proof of this sensitivity. The questions raised by the above statement are multitudinous and the avenues of possible research, study, and documentation are legion.

4. Is George always right? The answer here again is definitely No. George is not always right. I have suggested that his accuracy is about 80 percent. This figure I hope to gradually refine and understand.

The real answer to the question must be seen in terms of George's humanity. Some days he is tired, distracted, disinterested, or perhaps even frightened. Such factors will decrease his accuracy or even delay or put off an interview. In the case of a barrette studied, his report bore no relationship to the facts. It would appear that neither George nor his informants are infallible.

As in the case with other psychics, George is a specialist. He is interested in Indians, and it is in this area that his pronouncements prove to be more accurate, and the area in which he exhibits the most interest and enthusiasm.

5. Can his ability be tested and verified? The answer to this is definitely Yes. I have already done a great deal of this and hope to see the results in book form for comment and study.

But the real crunch comes in endeavouring to cope with George's excavation advice. George not only deals with artifacts, but he is sensitive to archaeological sites as well. Upon a site he almost quivers and comes alive like a sensitive bird dog scenting the prey.

He has given me enough advice on where to dig and what I will find to keep me busy for a decade.

At the same time, George's statements can be tested against published site reports and ethnohistoric and ethnological knowledge.

This, then, is *intuitive archaeology: a psychic approach.* It is a new approach, and it offers a new source of knowledge about man's prehistory. In this area of parapsychological research, I ponder my next step. In my first encounter with George, I responded with what I choose to call open-minded skepticism. Since that time, my study and immersion in things parapsychological has been diverse, intensive, and even broadening.

My initial feelings were of discovery, uniqueness, and, I assure you, loneliness, with a sense of mission that my role was to demonstrate, document, and reveal to the world the reality of George's intuitive ability and also the verification of his knowledge, which has now taken a continuing but secondary priority.

I am now aware that scientists and scholars of all kinds, psychologists, doctors, biologists, physicists, chemists, authors, and churchmen of all creeds, in all parts of the world, are emerging with new and vital interpretations and data which have elevated the discipline and study of the parapsychological to the realm of the acceptable and the inferential.

[This awareness was a considerable revelation to one so innocent. Moreover, it became vividly evident that their broad, shared aim seemed to be to contribute to the understanding of man, his nature, his universe, and perhaps to his ultimate purpose. Also in Dr. Emerson's papers was this description of his interpretation of what happened after his first paper was given:]

I have pondered about an adequate descriptive word and have decided that the best way to put it is to say that my talk was "graciously" received. There was prolonged, pointed, and vigorous discussion. Many questions were asked and, I believe, answered with at least some degree of success. The same or similar questions have been asked of George and me since that time on numerous occasions.

It was not until six months had passed that the following communication came to me in mid-September:

It might interest you to know that the lecture which you

gave at SFU this spring and at which I was fortunate to be present, was packed with people who had come to get a few laughs. It was interesting to watch the doubters emerge looking pretty thoughtful, and I was unable to find anyone who would seriously challenge your presentation. From what I had been told to expect, I was expecting to hear some rather interesting arguments in the bar afterwards. I heard none, nor was I able to learn of any. Doubters there no doubt were, but I suspect they found their cause unpopular.

I am very grateful for receiving such a communication and hope to be forgiven if I preserve the writer's anonymity. I have heard that some individuals were quite disturbed by what they heard. This is very understandable because some cherished beliefs were being challenged in a subtle way. A rather mysterious world was being presented to them for consideration; and the mysterious can be quite frightening, I assure you.

The majority of mature, conservative, scientifically-oriented colleagues were congratulatory. They shook my hand and thanked me for a most interesting and thought-provoking talk. But they did it with a wry smile and a twinkle in their eyes. They were by no means convinced and I suspect they wondered if it were some kind of put-on. They were not sure whether I was really serious or what would follow next. They naturally expected more proof and hard data.

As might be expected, the most positive response came from the younger people. To them I feel a great obligation, for they were quite ready to accept my statement of faith. I hope that what has followed helped to confirm their belief in my seriousness and sincerity. The young were eager to hear more and to exchange experiences and confidences. Many rather mysterious psychic happenings were told to me and at least one young man confided to me that he regularly went into trance to locate archaeological sites.

It was rather exciting for me when he was able to meet my friend George and that they confirmed each others' psychic knowledge of a site in Yoho National Park. The encouragement of these young people was most helpful to me and I am grateful to them.

It only gradually dawned upon me that I had made a decision which had brought me to the point of no return and that from then on matters could only get better or worse. Such is the nature of a public commitment; and one had obviously been made.

The next most positive response was the one to be expected:

namely, a test. At the banquet the following evening, George and I were presented with a black argillite stone carving for George to psychometrize. The reception had been a cocktail party and was, to say the least, festive and free-flowing and George had participated fully. The carving was presented to us by a local non-professional whom neither of us had ever met. I asked the donor to provide me with no details upon the object in order to avoid the suspicion that George might read my mind and gain such knowledge. So it was definitely a test and a challenge.

In actual fact, little was known about the artifact and it had been the subject of much speculation. As an anthropologist and especially as an archaeologist, I felt that there were certain things about it that I could say: it was argillite, which meant that the material must have come from the Queen Charlotte Islands. It was carved, but it certainly was not art in the Northwest Coast tradition. To me it certainly appeared to be a carved head or more accurately the profile of a face. But it was the face of an ape or perhaps that of an early fossil man at the pithecanthropus level of human development.

It was not until much later that the possibility of its representing the Sasquatch or the Abominable Snowman occurred to my wife, who has no psychic pretensions. It also seemed to me that the head had been carved in such a way that the structure had been weakened and had broken off from the body of the object. These were my immediate speculations and I am sure that they were not novel.

The reader can imagine my chagrin at the banquet when the first thing George had to say about this artifact was that it had been carved by a black man from Port Au Prince in the Caribbean. He seemed to be involved with the wrong race and the wrong part of the world to make any sense. At that point I decided to wait until the next day when the effects of the reception had worn off.

However, the next morning George reiterated his statements and added more that made it seem even more unlikely. So I decided George was out of his home territory and that it was best to put off further study of the artifact until we returned to Ontario where it seemed to me at that time George's expertise lay.

I have since, over many months, collected some 70 pages of text on this artifact. George expanded and enlarged upon his original assessment. He insisted on his first evaluation that it had been carved by a black man from Africa.

George told me that this black man had been captured as a slave and brought to the New World—to Port Au Prince. He had later been purchased by the British and taken on a ship around the tip of South America to the B.C. Coast where he escaped; in time, he met the natives, married, had children, and died there. Among other things, he had carved this artifact.

Now that is a fascinating story, yet it was not one that I could very well take back to my colleagues. But then strange events began to happen. Like so many things that have come about since I took up this study, there seemed to be some kind of synchronicity at work.

It began to feel almost like my work was being led. My daughter Lynn came back from Europe to be married at our home. Her university roommate came to see her; Sandy read tarot cards. It occurred to me that if she could do that, maybe she could psychometrize. She did not know whether she could or not. I gave her an artifact and she laid out the cards and proceeded to give me a very good reading. She later said that it was like seeing moving pictures and knowings that came into her head and she would describe or relay them to us.

When I handed her the carving, Sandy, too, saw the carver as coming from West Africa and being brought here as a slave. She described a number of things that George had not spoken of, yet she, too, saw him taken to British Columbia and escaping from his captors. But she added another dimension to the story. She insisted she saw a big, hairy, red-brown ape man going about his business.

The next happening in the chronicle of events was that my sister Mary told me she felt her husband Jim might be able to psychometrize, because he would tell her things that there was no way he could have known, yet that proved true. Sure enough, when Jim held the artifact he gave me a similar story about a black man being taken from West Africa as a slave, brought to the New World and later going to B.C. I didn't realize it then, but my second paper was in the works.

I feel that this first test of George's abilities has been met with considerable success. I am grateful to the donor who allowed me to take the carving home and work with it. It has led to developments which were, at the time, beyond even my wildest expectations, as witnessed by the development of what I now call a "psychic team" and my own expanded learning in this whole parapsychological area.

In a positive way, I am also grateful to the members of the Archaeological Society of British Columbia, who invited me to submit my article for publication in *The Midden* even though the editor prudently pointed out that my views were "not necessarily those of the Society." This led to further publicity and more tests that were forthcoming.

In summation of this point of no return, I have found the whole experience rewarding and a stimulus to go forward rather than to recant. Events which followed have abetted my developing resolution to continue. Moreover, in the mysterious way that things have increasingly tended to happen, it was brought to my attention that neither I nor those who were in the lecture hall that afternoon were by any means alone. It was indicated to me by someone who can see auras and spirit presences that the spirit attendance was quite substantial. Moreover, they apparently enjoyed the presentation, probably because it in some subtle way included them. It is possible they enjoyed it more than the visible audience did. Naturally I was pleased to be told I had such support.

Chapter 4

Comments by George

Dr. Emerson and his wife Ann had come to my home in Peterborough, Ontario, to stay over New Year's weekend. Norm took this opportunity to try—or test—my ability to psychometrize some artifacts he had brought with him. There were four of us present: Norman, Ann, my wife Charlotte, and me. We sat around the kitchen table and Norman produced a broken piece of pipe stem. I explained to him where he had found it, what the completed pipe had looked like, and how old it was.

I then drew a picture of what the missing pipe bowl had looked like. He was noncommittal through all of this and had no comments, only questions. He then showed me a human effigy pipe, which I again told him about and drew a picture with the missing portions intact. He appeared very excited by this time and plied me with more and more questions.

His questions became more and more difficult and careful as the time went by, as though he wanted to get all the information he could. I could see that he was quite impressed with my answers. He then brought out a bag of coins and asked me to look at them. I told him they were from burials of later or Christian Indians and told him they were from the Holland Marsh area just north of Toronto. Two pennies had been used to cover the eyes of one dead person. One gold sovereign, found in the pocket of a man, I knew was treaty money he had kept for some reason known only to himself.

There were other coins that had an unpleasant association, but the main thing was that the burials were of one family group and that they had died from some type of disease, which I named as being smallpox at the time. They had been discovered by a man digging the foundation for a new house. Norman found this site very distasteful and so did I.

The fact that Dr. Emerson had himself been the archaeologist who excavated these sites enabled him to know their story and be able to, at the time, assess the accuracy of my statements. He was still very skeptical, but he had to admit that I had described what he had seen or knew to be true. He realized he would have to digest this and make arrangements for further studies. He had no intention of accepting this new discipline without a lot of convincing and further testing.

Chapter 5

The Holland Landing Coins
An Unpublished Paper by Dr. Emerson

*[Of the unpublished papers Dr. Emerson left behind, his wife
Ann has given me one that dealt only with the coins he gave me
at the end of the first psychometry session, and which obviously
deeply impressed him. It tells, as well, his view of that first fateful
time when we brought together our individual talents and expresses
his feelings as he began his quest away from cold, academic investigation into this new, uncharted field of inquiry. His unpublished
paper follows.]*

The backhoe operator excavating a cellar for what was to be
Harvey Graham's new house near Holland Landing, north of Toronto, made only a few cuts before he stopped. He killed the engine,
got down from the machine, and looked at the contents of the
bucket. There was earth there, of course, but there were other things
which caused him to run for Graham and which caused Graham
to run for his wife and then the authorities: human bones, bits of
wooden coffin, a few decayed pieces of homespun, some leather,
skull fragments, and a long braid of glossy black hair. Graham
remembered the hair most of all, for there was something grotesque
about that hair that had grown from a scalp which had long since
decayed.

Graham, naturally, wanted the stuff out of there. He wanted to
get on with the building of his house and he'd rather not, he thought,
have the cellar floor pressing down on human remains—no point
in having the place haunted right from the start. Archaeologists
were called in. As the senior archaeologist at the University of
Toronto's Department of Anthropology and something of an expert
on Ontario Iroquois history and prehistory, I was asked to supervise
an emergency salvage excavation.

Eventually it was necessary to expand the operation well beyond the house foundations itself. Controlled, systematic digging revealed a series of burial pits. These we dug inch by inch, recording and photographing as we went. All the dirt piles were sifted by hand; we were determined to miss nothing.

The bodies—and there were quite a number of them—had been buried in rough pine caskets held together with square, hand-wrought nails. This meant that these Indians were living with the whites and were probably Christians, although there were no records in the local archives to substantiate this. One elderly man who had always lived in the vicinity said that when he was a boy playing on the site there were wooden stubs in the ground, on which one could trip, which could have been the bases of crosses. Most of the burials were individual, but there were also clusters of coffins in common graves. Many were infants, their tiny caskets placed directly on top of larger ones, presumably their parents'. There was something unnatural about the site. The skeletons showed evidence of hurried burial, as if most of the deaths had taken place near the same time. The burials were all Indian.

There was no evidence of violent death. Our guess was that this site, previously unrecorded as a burial ground, was the focus for native victims of one of the many plagues that swept across southern Ontario in the 1800s, sometimes wiping out whole villages.

All the members of the field team, as well as the Grahams, had a queasy feeling about the place. I certainly felt it. I remember at one point looking up from a position on my knees in one of the graves—I had just picked up a scrap of decayed leather—and seeing a group of Indians from a nearby reserve standing by the fence, quietly watching. None of them moved or said anything, yet I could feel the prickling hostility behind their brooding gaze, and for the first time in more than 30 years of digging I felt like a common grave robber. I shook the feeling off and went back to work, but it continued to haunt me long afterwards.

The other thing that upset me about the site—as it had Harvey Graham earlier—was the hair: that glossy black hair, tangled up in skull bones and dirt and fragments of nondescript leather. We felt, for no good reason, repelled by it. It is not our custom to dig any recent burials or those where the natives had been connected with white civilization and this was the first time we had found hair with the skulls we excavated. We would not have dug the site had it not been considered salvage work and had we not been requested to do so by the owner.

We found some grave goods from the historic period, including eight coins. There were four gold English sovereigns in almost mint condition, recovered from what had been the breast pocket of the owner's fragmented leather jacket. They were dated 1824 to 1838. There were two silver dollars, dated 1845 and 1846, found in what had been the pants pocket of an adult male. Two copper pennies, badly eroded, had been placed over the eyelids of a third person—an infant. On only one of these was the date discernible: 1820.

Two coppers on a dead child's eyes. Two silver dollars. Four shiny gold sovereigns. There seemed nothing particularly bizarre about the eight coins, nothing to make them especially memorable— unless it was the uniformly uneasy feeling the site gave the search party. I have been a long time in this business, and any archaeologist who has been active for some time digs up literally thousands of archaeological trinkets, ranging from pieces of ordinary and also lovely pottery vessels to almost unrecognizable fragments of iron, leather, bone, and stone. But what I know now about those coins makes them stand out vividly in my memory.

For what I discovered through them has opened up for me a dizzying series of possibilities, changing me from an elderly, cautious, conservative scholar into. . .into what? Something of an explorer, I guess—a searcher in a field which seems to me genuinely new and open. It is sentimental, but not false, to say that those eight coins, buried hastily on a southern Ontario plain more than a hundred years ago, helped set my life off on a new course. And, I believe, these changes will have repercussions far beyond my own modest reputation.

It was another five years before I met George, that fascinating, complex man who was to come to play such a large role in my life and its changes. And it was another year after that before I brought George and the Holland Landing coins together, thereby acting as the catalytic agent for those very changes.

It all began quite haphazardly. My wife Ann was a member of a women's study group investigating the whole range of psychic phenomena. George's wife Charlotte was a member of the same group. The two women, who discovered they felt the same way about a good many things, soon became fast friends and saw a good deal of each other.

I took little part in their explorations. As I said, I was a fairly elderly scholar—I was 56—enjoying a position of reasonable respect within my profession. I had most of the required accouter-ments of academia—two master's degrees, a doctoral degree

(University of Chicago) a full professorship, tenure, an academic history of some dedication, a comfortable salary. I was somewhat of an authority on the Iroquois. I had a list of papers and publications to my name and a few other accomplishments. It is not a brilliant history, but it is a sound one.

Psychic phenomena were quite foreign to this background. It would not be right to say at this point that I was skeptical of psychics; they had never impinged on my consciousness enough for me to generate so much as skepticism. They lived, almost literally, in another world.

When Ann's interest in the subject deepened, I did some reading. I read a little of Dr. J.B. Rhine, the Duke University researcher who is known as the founder of American parapsychology and whose meticulous experiments with extra-sensory perception (a word he coined) used science's own methods to prove statistically that more than chance operated in connection with psychic work. I perused some of Arthur Koestler's writings. I read about a few of the famous psychics. I looked into the records of some of the more respected ones. I became aware of the serious work being done and also of the charlatans the field attracts.

Still, it was all fun and games. It was not serious. It was not, in a fundamental sense, *real.*

Ann also discovered that her friend's husband, George, was regarded as a psychic and that in addition to the more usual psychic "gifts," he was able to do "readings" for people, offering "helpful insights" and occasionally predicting the future. (George has since abandoned this practice; he says it depresses him too much to bring bad news to people he likes.) When Ann met him, he was doing readings only for relatives and close friends, and then only under prompting from his wife. For some reason he must have considered me a friend, although we had never met. More likely he did it for Ann at his wife's request.

In 1970 I was not well, and after an upsetting session on an Ouija board in which there were dire predictions for my health, Ann asked if George would do a reading for me. He did not know me at all, and he asked Ann only my height and weight. (He later told Ann that he was aware that he had known me in another life and that he knew we would be working together.)

In essence and without going into much detail, I will say that George did highlight what was wrong with my health. It matched what the doctors had been telling me and impelled me to overcome my stubbornness and take the recommended treatment. Much later,

George clearly predicted a change in residence for us from the house we had occupied for 24 years, at a time when we had no inkling of change. The move took place a year later.

Were these games or more than games? I was intrigued, I think, but no more.

It was inevitable, then, since our wives were friends, for George and me to meet. We did so quite naturally, without special emotion, and soon became close friends. In fact, we were almost automatically good friends, it seems—fishing, boating, card-playing, beer-drinking friends. And although we were friends, I was not aware of George's abilities or that he was the one who had "read" about my physical condition. It was many months before I discovered that he had the power to "psychometrize."

Psychometry is a word stolen from psychiatry; in its psychic meaning it is the ability to investigate and analyze an object or artifact by psychic means; to contemplate an object and intuit its history, its maker, its owner, and much other information—all the bits of its history which apparently had clung to it in all the years of its "beingness."

It required no great flash of insight to realize that I, as an archaeologist, was in a unique position to provide George with historical artifacts and at the same time, through my archaeological and anthropological training, was in an excellent position to test his findings. Archaeologists are always wondering, of course, who made the artifacts they discover. Their whole science is one of painstaking detective work, piecing together small fragments of evidence in attempts to make coherent pictures of vanished cultures.

If George could tell me intuitively who made the items, what kind of people they were, and what they were thinking while making them, not only would this help my work, but it would provide me with a richly-textured picture of the past previously quite out of my reach. What endless possibilities this would open up for my profession. . .

I was determined to give George representative artifacts. I selected, among other things, the coins found on Harvey Graham's property: those found along with the bits of leather, intact human skulls, and glossy black hair. The hair had been haunting me, and perhaps that is why I chose those coins.

It was still a game, though. Definitely a game.

By this time I had learned a great deal more about George himself, whose anonymity I continued to protect. He was born in 1920 in a small town near Toronto and has spent almost all of his life in Ontario (though recently he moved to British Columbia). As far as he can remember, he has always had the abilities he now demonstrates—the power to know the thoughts of obscure, long-dead people; the ability to read character and, in some degree, to read the future.

Before he learned how to read in school, George *knew* the white man had persecuted the Indian in Canada and then written his histories to make the Indians out to be the savages. His informants, George considered, were incontrovertible—they were *there*. This was also before he learned that his great-grandmother on his father's side was an Ojibwa—a distant connection, but one of which he is proud.

When George was young and apparently incorrigible (he was sent home from school the first day for refusing to stand for "God Save The King," then the Canadian National Anthem) he would sometimes go into trance. His mother called in the local minister, whom George remembers with distaste. The minister told George he was on the way to hell, and George retorted that it would be fine with him, for at least he'd be with the heathen "savages" and not the Christian liars and hypocrites.

The other kids, George remembers, always thought he was crazy when he told them things that had happened a long time before or things which were going to happen. One summer day in 1934, when George was 14, a friend of about the same age left to spend a vacation with an uncle near the town of Kirkland Lake. After he had gone, George turned to the other boys and said, "We'll never see him again." As usual he was derided. Later that summer, as the boy was hitchhiking home, he was struck and killed by a car. Still—and this says something for the cussedness of human disbelief—no one took George seriously. He was given the impression that they felt as if he were somehow responsible for the death.

At about this time, George recalls, he began keeping his foreknowledge to himself. He'd already shed the trance state and could exercise his abilities with little apparent change in appearance. (He demonstrated this for me and I saw what he meant: he looks rather like a man who is intent on something and who is concentrating deeply. His voice takes on a more guttural quality; his choice of words and phrases becomes slower, more deliberate. There is little other change.)

It was a moral decision he made about not telling people the future. It is painful for him to know that someone close to him is going to die, but this is not the only reason: he appreciates just how much influence he could have—the danger of prophecies becoming self-fulfilling is real. If he told someone he or she would get ill, and that person believed him, it would be likely that the illness might come about because of it. A good psychic, George insists, will keep his mouth shut. "We have no right to interfere in people's lives, to plant the seeds of thoughts in somebody's mind."

George cooperates with me partly because of the excitement of the chase, partly because we are good friends, and partly because he feels my academic reputation will help him get across a story he wants told—the story of the essential goodness of the Indian and his culture.

George himself uses the word *Native* instead of Indian and is most vehement in his view of what he sees as the callous, inhuman, and evil treatment accorded the Indians by the whites. At the same time, George harbours a deep contempt for white arrogance and for English ways in particular.

When he was young, he had a perfect attendance at Sunday School for a whole year. As a reward he was given a flashlight—and it didn't work. This may have had some influence on his feeling about churches. He dislikes also the established churches, and more particularly the Jesuits, though he does not count himself an atheist. He understands and respects the ways of the Ontario Indian before the time of white settlement.

I mention George's prejudices as well as his abilities because I want you to get a picture of my co-researcher at this point. None of this is "scientific." Everything I have said about George is open to various interpretations, is often ambiguous, uncheckable—inherently unscientific. I felt the same way, I assure you. George was a fascinating man with fascinating stories. He was a warm man and a good friend. I couldn't disbelieve him, exactly, because he *was* a friend, yet I didn't precisely believe him, either. I was in a state of suspended belief. Or suspended disbelief—I didn't know which.

It was, as I said, still a game.

It was January 1, 1971, and very cold. We were in George's kitchen. I pushed the Holland Landing coins across the table toward my friend. He reached out, took them, and spread them out on the table, touching them lightly in sequence. This was the first time I had "worked" with George, though he had already read some other artifacts for me at this session. I wish I could say now I had been prescient, that I expected something important, but I'm afraid I didn't. As nearly as I can recall it, my mood was one of open-minded interest, willing to judge by the outcome.

A sort of game, but a fascinating one.

There were just the four of us at that kitchen table in George's house near Peterborough, Ontario—Ann and I, George and Charlotte. George preferred working in his own kitchen to anywhere else; there he was surrounded by familiar objects and comfortable moods without distractions. Three of us sat at the table. Charlotte stood behind George; he used her, he said half jokingly, as his "psychic battery"—and indeed, after a long session her face would go quite pale with the strain, for she generously made available her quiet but considerable energy.

George tapped the coins again. Then two—the silver dollars—he pushed away from him. They offended him for some reason. "They paid for something that shouldn't be," he explained.

"What?"

He shrugged. "Slavery involved? They bought flesh, anyhow, is my feeling. I don't like them, they bother me." He pushed them further away. "They make me angry. Either they bought flesh or someone was killed for them. Loss of dignity or life involved here. Revolting. Could be prostitution involved." He picked up one of the pennies. "What is it?"

"A copper penny."

He paused, puzzled, handled it, thought, listened, heard nothing. "It has deteriorated too badly. In itself, it's gone. No life. I can't feel the life in it. There is not time in it—no life. Fairly recent, like the others. No more than 100 years."

He listened again to the penny, but still heard nothing but the years themselves, echoing hollowly down the time line. Time without content. He could pick up nothing at all about it.

George leaned forward, pushed the silver dollars still further away. They still bothered him. He picked up the smaller gold sovereigns. He felt nothing dishonest there. "Normal barter, except for circumstances where they were found," he said.

"Where were they found?"

"With someone dead who owned them. Sault comes to mind. Not Sioux—S-A-U-L-T. Tuberculosis. Person died of it. Other stuff, too, not just these. Uncanny. Around Georgian Bay somewhere. Inland. Normal session. Not dishonest. Smell of death. Tuberculosis. For the big coins, I feel only revulsion. Big coins stolen from someone. Cost him his life. A him, who lost his life.

"Funny thing, uncanny. I see hair. I can see black hair. The hair of dead people still there. Unpleasant. I want to say, near Bradford. Two adults and a young child. Not too far from the bend of the river—bed of an old lake. It was dug with a team—with a scoop when digging post holes."

There was more, but that was the substance of this part of the psychometry. I have no tape of the session—systematic research hadn't yet begun—and I am indebted to the careful notes Ann took while George spoke. I believe the quotes are accurate.

I remember leaning back in my chair, impressed. More, it is fair to say, I was astounded. Sure there were things about George's statements which could never be checked. There was no way of telling whether those silver dollars had ever been used for some less than reputable purpose. There was no way of finding out for sure whether the owner had died of tuberculosis, though clearly illness was responsible for the mass graves and tuberculosis was not an impossible diagnosis. George had only said that the possessor of the coins had died of it.

There were a few things which were clearly wrong—it was a backhoe, not a "team" which had uncovered the coins; it was for a cellar, not "post holes." But these seemed minor points. Some of the other evidence was impressive! I looked again at Ann's notes.

George could have spotted the dates on the coins, though he didn't appear to do more than touch them, so his assessment of "not much more than 100 years" was not too surprising. The natives were most probably either Mississauga or Ojibwa who were in the area at this time, and this is consistent with the mention of the Sault, since the Sault Ste. Marie area was occupied by both groups and was a point from which their southern migrations had taken off. More importantly, George had placed the location of the find to within a few miles—Bradford is only two or three miles from Holland Landing. And this with the whole world to choose from! This was, already, surely beyond the bounds of guesswork.

The site was quite precisely pinpointed: it was indeed located in a bend of the Black River which flows from the fertile plain called Holland Marsh into Lake Simcoe and ultimately into Georgian Bay. Moreover, the flat, sandy ground where the Grahams were building their home was once the bottom of a lake.

And the hair—that is what rivetted me. George saw and was upset by the long, black hair that had turned up with the skulls. No one had mentioned hair to him. More: no one had told him the coins had been found with skeletons, yet he saw the hair and the bodies and the place in the ground where they were laid, finally, to rest. . .

George "psychometrized" a number of other objects for me that day. He was in a good mood and made the most of this appreciative audience. He "read" an heirloom-type bracelet for Ann and some other archaeological artifacts I had brought. Again, much of what he had to say was either vague or uncheckable, and in some cases where he did provide data I didn't have enough information to test his results. He seemed to know a lot more about Ann's heirloom than she did, for instance (she had bought it in an antique shop, and she had no way of knowing whether what he said was true).

Yet where George did mention verifiable facts, as in the session with the coins, his accuracy that afternoon ran to about 80 percent—a phenomenally good record even had he been a trained archaeologist and ethnographer, which I knew he was not. This 80-percent figure, which was to recur later, was both reassuring and tremendously upsetting. It meant, of course, that George was probably wrong 20 percent of the time, yet it still seemed disturbingly clear that the rest of his performance which was accurate was beyond the possibility of coincidence, luck, or guesswork.

Suddenly it didn't seem quite so much like fun and games any more.

In the car on the way home that afternoon, I brooded. I was, as I said, impressed, upset—and very cautious. The whole weight of my academic experience militated against accepting this. . .this. . .performance. All my life I have been dedicated to cautious, painstaking analysis of fragmentary information, careful never to extrapolate beyond the evidence, nor to make assumptions not fully supported by the data.

Archaeology attracts careful, systematic people. Anyone who has watched them at work or who has taken part in a dig will know this. Not for us the dreaming of dreams, not for us the careless wielding of shovels. We get down into the dirt and do the digging carefully by feel with our hands, noses, and eyes, using great care and loving attention to detail.

I had never dealt with a psychic before. I had no idea how one worked. I had no way of judging his ability or reliability. I had no idea, then, how George did what he said he did—what he appeared to do. I didn't have a clue.

I didn't know whether he felt the vibrations in the artifacts, or traveled back into their past, or contacted the "spirits" on "the other side" who fed him information or what he did. All this was new to me and made me uneasy.

And God knows there were charlatans enough in this business. How could one be sure? Sure that one wasn't simply gullible?

George was a friend, and in any case didn't have the feel of a charlatan. He was too matter-of-fact about what he was doing. There was no hocus pocus, no phoney ritual. He seemed not to care whether or not he was believed. There was no payment or money involved. This was all worth considering.

It was his results which really got to me. A scientist, unless he is a mere dogmatist, must accept the evidence of his senses, his instruments, and his knowledge. He cannot simply pretend it isn't there, or hope that it will go away, tempting as that may be at times.

Here I was, an elderly person, stuck with an 80-percent figure which seemed to prove something I had known all my life was impossible. I was not yet convinced, I assure you, not at all. I wanted to eliminate all the other possibilities first. I wanted a good many more experiments—more hard data—before I would commit myself. Yet there was, I admit, a sudden unfolding of excitement, too, as George told me things about those coins which I *knew* to be true. It was the kind of excitement the young are said to experience when their minds are still open.

If this were for real and if George could do what he said he did—could be consistent and would agree to work with me in areas where I had enough expertise to test his results—what avenues would be open! Caution—native caution—stopped me there, but still. . .there in the car on the long drive home from that first session I saw a vision of the past opening up to me—opening up as it had done for no one else.

I would be risking my professional neck, of course, but if I were right it would open up whole new bodies of data for scientific scrutiny. It would be a new blend of the parapsychological and the hard sciences. A whole new discipline: intuitive archaeology. A study of the past by means of psychic informants.

I remember chuckling, and then I put it out of my mind for a while. I wasn't completely convinced that the games were over.

Chapter 6

Quackenbush and Other Sites
An Unpublished Paper by Dr. Emerson

[A second unpublished paper tells Dr. Emerson's own thoughts on the unfolding of our work together.]

We did little with this "intuitive archaeology" in the next while. George and I continued to be friends, but he was now in Peterborough, 80 miles from Toronto, so it was not so easy to get together. I was busy with my teaching and other duties and didn't have much time for further experimentation.

I had decided, however, that I wanted to pursue the matter further, for George's performance had intrigued me sufficiently that I couldn't put it out of my mind altogether—which would, I think, have been the more comfortable approach. It wasn't until the following summer that, almost by accident, George, archaeology, and I were brought together again. Once more a burial pit was responsible—a pit containing some strange and archaeologically erratic features.

Almost two decades ago, an Iroquois village was found on a farm, belonging to Lyle Quackenbush, near Peterborough, Ontario. Initial archaeological investigations were inconclusively carried out at the time and these were followed at intervals by small additional digs, mainly supervised by personnel from Trent University, a small college in Peterborough.

In the summer of 1972, the Provincial Ministry of Natural Resources began to take an interest in the site; there was a suggestion that it would be included as part of the development of a provincial park system which would centre on the widely-known and spectacular site called the Peterborough Petroglyphs. A small dig was underway at Quackenbush, supervised by a Peterborough history teacher, Robert Gordon, who had trained with me.

During the course of this dig, they uncovered a shallow mass grave. Most of the field team were still students, but they knew enough to see that there was something very odd about it. They called for outside help.

The Iroquois served their dead in two ways. The so-called primary burial was a simple, almost careless affair: the dead person was placed in the field on a scaffold, or in the woods in a crotch of a tree. Sometimes he was buried in a shallow pit or perhaps even deposited in the village garbage dump or buried under the floor of a longhouse if it was wintertime when the person died.

The secondary ("proper") burial took place much later, when the village moved or was abandoned. The dead were then collected, exhumed if necessary, and reburied in a communal burial pit or "ossuary" with great ceremony and honour. This burial took place with elaborate ritual and was called The Feast of the Dead or The Feast of the Kettle, often involving several hundred bodies.

What Gordon and his crew found was quite different. The burial pit was six and a half feet long, four feet wide, and a few feet deep. It contained 13 or 14 bodies. All had been stretched out and laid face down (a practice reserved for enemies). Four were children. Most had fractured bones at the base of the skull.

The Historical Sites and Parks Branch of the Ontario Ministry of Natural Resources—the provincial authority in such matters— asked me if I would have a look at the grave to see if I could come up with an interpretation. Since the site was not far from Peterborough, I decided to combine the trip with a visit with George. So it was a geographic accident that caused me to first take George to a dig; I had no idea he was sensitive to sites as well as to artifacts. It simply hadn't occurred to me.

It turned out to be fascinating. On a site, George seems almost to quiver and come alive. He is a man of some energy anyway, and on a site he would go charging off in some direction, only to stop, change direction, stop again, point, stop—all this with me trailing behind, at first with a clipboard, sketch pad, and surveyor's pins, later with a tape recorder.

He would move from point to point, stop, indicate where I should dig. "Here," he would say. "A rich spot. Burials. Dig here." Or, "The palisade wall came through here, better dig here." Then he would march off again, flinging off asides, observations, generalizations, moral judgments, value judgments, general observations on the site's history and human makeup, on its age and customs.

Several times during that first tour I sat down to rest, quite exhausted, while George charged off to explore some more. I was soon to recognize this feeling; it happened every time I was on a site with George. I'm pretty fit and don't exhaust easily. I certainly hadn't done enough that day to account for my weariness. It was only later that I remembered Charlotte's face in George's kitchen, and how he jokingly referred to her as his "psychic battery." Charlotte would go quite white as George, in some strange fashion "drew on her energy"; perhaps he was doing the same thing to me? I filed this away for further study under the general heading: "Unproved But Disturbingly Possible."

Nor is this activity always easy on George. He often receives impressions, he says, which are offensive or disgusting to him. Sometimes these impressions are so powerful ("like being hit by a lightning bolt," he has told me) that he cannot turn them off, and if they are evil or disgusting he will move away. On the only visit he ever paid to a museum, he was so repelled by the evil character of one of the mummies that he fled the building and never went back.

Certainly on archaeological sites I have seen him walk rapidly away from a spot, giving no explanation. Later he may or may not tell me what had upset him. If something took place in one of those villages 800 years ago that he considers an atrocity, he is quite likely to keep the details to himself; as a researcher I have just had to come to terms with the fact that George makes a good many moral decisions about what I should know.

On the Quackenbush site, as we shall see, George saw evidence of massacre and torture, and it upset him. I also have on tape his words as he stood on another site, known to archaeologists as the Boyes site. He had stopped abruptly, after walking rapidly around the site. "The burials are here. . .I can feel it underneath my foot. . .The worst thing happened right here. . ." He gave a long series of choking coughs, and his face went quite red, then white. "My throat. . .it almost feels like they were hung. . ." He would say no more that day and we left the site after only a cursory examination.

Quackenbush was for me a fascinating and infuriating experience. George provided me with so much advice and digging instructions that it would take years to make even a superficial check of them all. In addition, much of the other information he provided was ambiguous, inherently uncheckable, and, while interesting, relatively useless, scientifically uncheckable—the same as was often true of his psychometry of objects. I emerged from the session at Quackenbush encouraged, discouraged, puzzled, exhausted, and fascinated. (Together, of course, these words make up "confused" and that about sums it up.)

There was no one on the site when we arrived. It was evident that the skeletons had been removed. I was disappointed at not being able to view them, but obviously time and weather conditions had impelled Gordon to get them out. I expected the burial pit would attract George's attention, but he seemed to have no reaction to it. He certainly made no comment. He seemed more interested in an area toward the north of the site.

We walked slowly northwards, climbing over a fence, finally reaching a high point where George quested about and (as I learned later) got his bearings. It seems that when on a site George goes all over it to get an orientation of what is there and how things are in present time. Then it is as if he goes through a warp in time. When he does that, he can no longer see the site as it is today. He is there seeing it as it was at the time the Indians were there. He sees their houses, palisades, and campfires. He often knows what they are doing and thinking.

When he comes back, he needs that orientation to pin down the things he has seen in the context of how the site is today. The trees will likely be different, there will have been no roads or fences. He has to know the lay of the land in order to make a translation to the present.

He called me over to a particular spot and pointed. "You'll find burials here," he said. The soil was sandy but had a fairly high gravel content, and I was not optimistic about his advice. He said there were eight bodies buried there and asked whether they could be in a circle. I assured him they could be and he looked relieved. "Could they be buried around garbage disposal areas?" he asked. Again I assured him they could, and, looking pleased with himself, he pointed out what he said would be a rich midden area. We continued northwards along a ridge. George pointed east and southeast. "That's where they lived," he said. No digging had been done there yet, but as an archaeologist surveying the site I would have made the same guess and tested for longhouse construction there.

George was fumbling to put a date to the village. "Not too old," he said at first, then stopped. It seemed there were two distinct groups occupying the site at different periods and he was trying to sort them out. The people living in the eastern sector were much older, he concluded. They were already there 850 years ago. He put the second group about 200 years later. He wasn't sure whether habitation was continuous. He saw no sign of white influence anywhere.

We moved further northwards, toward a hill strewn with rocks and boulders. George stiffened, went pale. His voice became jerky. "There was slaughter here," he said. "I can see the attacking horde pouring over the hill. Attack from the north. Violent death. Torture." He fell silent, wouldn't say any more, refusing to be drawn out. I was already exhausted and we returned to the excavation area, where I sat down to rest while George went off to survey the southern part of the site. He apparently found little to interest him there and returned.

I pointed to the excavation pit. I wanted to know what he thought. So far he had ignored it, not showing even the reaction of a casual visitor. "It's a grave," he said abruptly. I was taken aback. George didn't usually snap at me. He spoke as if it should have been obvious to me, which of course it was. "Someone has taken the bones, he said, still angrily." (Later he told me he had been angry because his informant had been annoyed at the intrusion of archaeologists.)

I asked George when the bones were removed. "Within ten or 15 years," he said. They had actually been gone only a few days; but I later discovered that ten and 15 years before had been the time of the initial archaeological penetrations of the site.

"How many bodies were there?"

"Six," said George. (There had been twice that many.) "One had a cracked skull." (Gordon had intimated the damage was more severe than that.)

All in all, it didn't seem like an impressive performance, even taking into account George's induced anger. I told him the skeletons had been gone only a few days. He seemed indifferent. In fact, his indifference to the whole area surprised me.

While we were looking over the excavation area, I discovered a patella, a human kneecap. To save time, I told George what it was and asked him if he could provide details. He was still short with me, still annoyed. "It's an innocent person, a female," was all he would say, shrugging it off.

Then, his voice rising: "These were a very peaceful people who were slaughtered, in contrast to the warriors who attacked them. A peaceful community, not warlike, very cooperative. A peaceful, intelligent people trying their best. They were not just savages."

We went on another foray, this time west of north to a steep bank well away from the midden excavations. "If I were digging, I'd dig right here," he said. "But up there, on the flat, there'd be more bodies than anywhere."

We walked up the hill to the flat ground. George paced it off, turned back toward me. He seemed quite excited, somewhat disoriented, certainly distraught. His eyes were closed. He asked me, in an urgent tone: "Is there a plateau over to my right?" It was almost as if he could not see or didn't want to see. I agreed there was.

We went directly there and George at once declared, "Dig here, I would dig here." My archaeological training led me to disagree. The area was marked by quite sterile groundhog holes and I was not impressed by its excavation potential. But George was quite agitated. "It's an exciting area," he said. "Very exciting. A storehouse, a storehouse of stuff. Some signs of the white man in this area, too."

We left the Quackenbush site in George's car soon afterwards. I was exhausted again and fully expected we would return to George's home. But he was still excited and he wanted to talk. There was a great deal of suspicion "on the other side" about the excavations, George told me. They were quite agitated.

Returning to an earlier theme, he repeated that they were an industrious, intelligent people. After a search for words, he came up with "domesticated." They were healthy. Their lives involved little competition. They were motivated by a broad community spirit. There was plenty to eat, plenty of game and fish. They were fishermen and hunters. He saw no evidence of "anything we would consider edible" being cultivated. As he put it, "no cultured crops."

The people, who had come out of the west, were more "Eskimo" Indian looking than Indian. Their eyes were definitely more slanted, more Mongol looking. Flat faces, dark skins. A little more squatty than the Indians. Well-fed, almost plump. Heavy legs and narrow feet. Heavily muscled, well-developed. The women were big-breasted.

"They wore little in the way of decoration like beads or pendants. They painted their bodies a lot with a bright red and a black chalky substance. The men decorated their arms, wrists, elbows, and shoulders. The women, mostly the stomach and hips. The men used mostly red, the women mostly black. They seemed to be oiled, well-oiled, wore little clothing.

"There were at most 300 people. At the time of the massacre, only about 150. They lived in not so much houses as lean-tos.

Wood was used but skins more. These people traded a lot, especially skins and stoneware. In return they got sticks."

I asked George what these "sticks" were, but he was just as puzzled as I was. They just looked like. . .sticks. He was silent for a long while as we drove along. The problems of the origin of the Quackenbush people was puzzling him. It seemed they had been part of a group "two days travel to the south," whose customs were different and were considered by them to be "barbaric." These customs included hillside burial, in which bodies were buried sitting down. The Quackenbush people had split off from this group.

How, then, had they come "out of the west, from the land of no-snow," as George had said earlier? George just shrugged. He didn't know.

What to make of all this? How to evaluate it? Was any of it verifiable? On a few things George was quite clearly wrong. The number of skeletons removed had been 13 or 14, not six. The dwellings were certainly more than lean-tos; evidence of longhouse construction had been found.

On the other hand, George had not known of the archaeological anomalies on the site, yet had clearly seen a massacre and had suggested we would find a grave with eight bodies in it. This matched very well our discoveries and suppositions about them.

The digging that followed our visit matched George's description very well, even where his guesses had seemed unlikely. Archaeologists found only two projectile points in the months of digging. This scarcity of weaponry supported George's claim that they were a peaceable group.

The abundance—indeed omnipresence—of a stone called amphibolite impressed the diggers. It is a stone used to make axe and adze blades. Gordon found much of it in "blank form" state—roughly shaped out, ready for trading purposes. Again, this matched George's version. The whole site gave evidence of an established trade relationship, though more work is still needed to establish George's claim of a trade in hides.

George's most contentious statement was the lack of agriculture. I found it hard to believe that such an obviously Iroquois village would not be cultivating squash, beans, and corn, all traditional Iroquois crops. And, in fact, Gordon found ample evidence of all three vegetables.

But on closer scrutiny, George's version remained possible. Very few corn cobs were found, only kernels. The Quackenbush area is on the Cambrian Shield north of Peterborough, an area which is agriculturally very unreliable. This fact, combined with the lack of corn cobs, made it possible that the vegetables had been obtained from the south in return for stone.

Later in the summer, a student collected and analyzed a series of pollen cores and, despite the fact that he encountered a considerable number of pollen grains of trees, plants, and grasses, he found only one "problematical" corn pollen grain. The analysis does tend to suggest that George was right.

The remaining sociological and social comment provided by George matched the archaeologists' findings pretty well. The detailed analysis and investigations of George's excavation advice will have to wait; he always gives me more to do than I can handle in just one lifetime.

Which left the human kneecap.

This presented real interest because it seemed like a quick test of George's ability. I wanted to locate the skeleton that was short a kneecap, obtain an age and sex determination (which can be done on the bones and skull), and match George's statement against it.

The skeletons had been turned over to Trent University for study. Dr. H.S. Helmuth, a physical anthropologist at Trent, was able to match the kneecap to the skeleton marked "Individual Eight." I asked Dr. Helmuth if he could make a sex determination and approximate the age.

"Clearly a female," he said. "Age between 27 and 32."

So far not so good. George had said she was an "innocent" female, and, using my traditional Western cultural values, I arbitrarily—and quite wrongly—assumed he meant she would be a girl of about 13 or so who could run faster than her male companions. I put it to George again and his response put my culturally biased assumptions to shame.

He went on to explain that the person had been mentally retarded and had not been able to fully experience life. The natives treated her as innocent, he said.

"Was she about 13 or so?"

"Oh, no," said George. "She was 28."

It was, I thought, a draw, a standoff. George was wrong on two small issues, quite probably right on the rest. The issues of substance—the major excavations—still awaited resolution. It was open to interpretation. A hostile critic—or even a skeptic—would be able to rationalize away everything George had said as a guess, as a product of prior knowledge, as a probability. I determined to reserve my opinion.

I was disappointed, I suppose, that the results didn't approximate the drama of the Holland Landing coins; but on the other hand, it seemed to me not unhopeful that if we could hit on a site where George was really "in tune" and where the archaeological checks were available, we might still be able to develop the method.

Our next effort, however, turned out to be even more confusing. I took George on a tour of the Huron town of Cahiague, once the capitol of Huronia—an immense place that covered hundreds of acres and once contained about 300 buildings, according to Champlain, who had visited the site in 1615. I had conducted student and summer digs there for more than ten years and had reason to want to know something definitive about the palisade.

George confessed that he was confused and disoriented on the site. He kept exclaiming at the vast numbers of Indians. He was unable to find any gravesites; he said he was confounded by the jostling, energetic crowds he saw everywhere. The "living" (to George) were crowding out the dead. He did manage to date correctly the village's founding; he got a pretty good figure for the number of people it contained and was able to provide, almost to the year, the date the town was finally abandoned by the Hurons (1838).

He was wrong on the number of buildings (when pressed, he thought there might be "as many as 250," but pointed out that his informants had never thought to count them). For the rest, he was sidetracked into an elaborate story of a party of 12 or 15 French voyageurs visiting the town and a discussion of how they had gotten there—an interesting story in itself, but of little value for my purpose at the time.

This was not an encouraging experience for our research. It was at this point that George tried to explain his "method," partly, I suspect, to get across to me why things occasionally went wrong. The method doesn't translate very well into scientifically-acceptable terminology, but bear with me.

George has three "guides" (I suppose the usual psychics or those who are mediums would call them "controls" or "familiars") on the "other side." He doesn't actually "see" them, but pictures them as being rather like glowing clouds, sexless, with "voices" neither young nor old. (The plethora of quotation marks here betrays the uneasiness I had with these terms.)

These voices become his guides, his travel agents, as it were, as he moves through time. They put him in touch, through some means about which George knows nothing, with the people in the villages he visits, who speak to him through some thought process akin, as near as he can tell it, to memory.

As George puts it, "Some of these memories are of things as they were when they were there, and they are not always accurate, either. This other world is just as confusing as our material world and you have to evaluate the good guys from the bad guys." Some people, it seems, still have axes to grind after seven centuries. Besides, their memories are selective and don't always cover the things which interest George or, for that matter, me.

Sometimes, if the contact is good, George is enabled to "see" things himself. "If I wanted to see something specific, like, say, the way people dressed for a certain ceremony, I would actually be able to see the ceremony in a detached way, like I was in a tree looking down on them." He gets temperatures, sounds and smells—but never touch or taste. What he sees, hears, and smells affects him emotionally, directly, and he experiences everything from tranquillity to revulsion. When he describes a scene he does so with the appropriate emotion.

With artifacts, he experiences temperatures directly. This is how he judges age—the older, the colder. I have discovered it can be remarkably accurate. Occasionally George will see things as if through a zoom lens. Indeed, when pinpointing a piece of geography or locating the origin of a site, this seems to be his method. I noticed it with the Holland Landing coins. First he located the general area, then narrowed the focus to "inland" and then zoomed in on the spot itself.

I also learned something which made me more cautious about insisting on getting answers. If George sees something that upsets him, the effects may stay with him for some time. The two silver dollars from Holland Landing caused him nightmares and it was weeks before he shook them off. He has an ability that brings with it consequences and is not to be taken too lightly.

At this point I could feel my interest was flagging a little. I was busy with many other projects.

I was becoming confused about what George could or could not do. I needed a demonstration. I needed to take George to a site more comfortable than the crowded Cahiague, which had intimidated him with its scale. I needed a site which was under investigation by archaeologists but was as yet relatively unmapped, leaving George with untouched areas. My best bet was the Boyes site, I thought.

The Boyes Site was a prehistoric Indian village located in what is now Pickering Township, east of Toronto. The archaeologist in charge was Paddy Reid, then a graduate student from McMaster University in Hamilton, Ontario.

Paddy's party had been engaged, in the weeks before we got there, in trying to locate the main palisade of the village. Although Paddy was still a graduate student, he knew enough to realize where the palisade should be—on the brow of the small hill. There was no other place for it.

He dug, and found nothing. He removed a thousand square feet of earth and more, and still found nothing.

George liked Paddy immediately, which seemed to put him "in tune" and determined to help. I had a tape recorder by this time, so I could record the conversation as Paddy wandered behind us, surveyor's pins in hand. It was a hot day in early summer and the Ontario black flies—the curse of bush work—were out in force.

George: "Black flies pretty thick around here."

Emerson: "They are, yeah. How are the 'vibrations' this morning?"

George: "They're pretty good. Not bad at all."

Emerson: "I was wondering about the diggers, you know, whether they are going to affect things."

George: "No, not particularly."

Emerson: "Some of them are positive, some are enthusiastic, some are negative. I was just wondering if we could move over before bodies arrive and have a look."

George: "At the barricade?"

Emerson: "Did this site have a palisade around it?"

George: "It didn't have a big one. They were at this end of the point and they just put the palisade across that way, just behind there." (He pointed.)

Emerson: "Oh, dear, you mean under that big dirt pile?"

George: "Yeah."

Emerson: "Would it run around here at all, George?" [That is, the perimeter of the site.]

George: "No, it came down a certain amount, but do you see where that maple is, there? Well, it came across there just a little bit, but then it ran across this way."

Emerson: "In other words, what they did was just palisade the back end of the village?"

George: "Yes, what they did was, they cut off the point."

Emerson: "And they didn't worry about it?"

George: "No, they didn't have to."

At this point he stooped, took up a stick, and scuffed a sketch into the dust. A straightish line cutting off a promontory, with little baffles on each end and a "gate," also baffled.

George: "That's the way it looked. Maybe a little more of an angle, like that; this of course here is at an angle like that and went down into the ravine."

Emerson: "So if we put a five-foot test trench or two in, we should be able to pick out the post holes, shouldn't we?"

George: "Yeah. Right there, not where that car is, but this side of it."

Emerson: "Could we walk on over there and maybe approximate it?"

George: "Walk over, walk over it so many times, they tried to plough it, had it for pasture, run tracks over it, and wet—oh this has been pounded down bad. Over there was worse because when it was wet they run through it a lot. You see a lot of humps like this you can't tell what the hell it's for, they tried to plough it. Right there, right across—see where this is over here, it runs down to right about there, then it cuts right straight through here, almost in a line with those. . .there, almost in line. . .with that."

Emerson: "So it's. . .oh, hell, if we put in a trench across here we are bound to hit it?"

George: "Yeah. Run a trench across here to almost here. You'll hit it. You'll find a palisade."

Paddy was still following us, placing white survey pins in the ground as indicated by George. Paddy and I looked back. From available archaeological evidence, the palisade simply couldn't be where George said it was. It was all wrong. They *wouldn't* have put a palisade there. . .

Paddy decided to dig anyway. He'd found nothing by any other method and at least this would be a test for George. He was looking for evidence of the palisade post holes. These show up as dark, circular soil stains, which contrast clearly with the surrounding sandy soil. They are the remains of the holes which once contained the palisade posts. Sometimes these posts burned or rotted away, but more routinely they were removed when the village relocated and the holes would fill with debris. Although post-hole patterns are well-known to archaeologists, they cannot be located in any way, even by experts, except by digging. George had never seen post-hole evidence before and was, in any case, no expert.

Paddy dug where George had indicated. He found the palisade. George was off by no more than five inches. It wasn't a lucky hit, either. The palisade followed the direction George said it would. Every twist and turn was there. George had seen it all. It was impossible.

More: At one point in the excavation, the holes seemed to disappear. George explained that there had been a baffle-like gateway there. He pointed out where Paddy should dig. Paddy dug. And there it was!

By the time the recording resumed, George's attention had turned to a dwelling house which he said was just within the palisade walls. We walked across the field and I emphasize that, even to a skilled eye, it was just an overgrown field, complete with long grass, weeds, and sumach bushes. There was literally no archaeological evidence to be seen. Paddy brought up the rear again with his survey pins.

Emerson: "In other words, it [the wall] is running east and west?"

George: "Yeah, the long part was that way, the narrow part this way."

Emerson: "That would make it about 60, 70 feet long?" [The somewhat usual length of longhouses where I had dug.]

George: "Oh, no, it seems to me it would be about 30 feet long."

Emerson: "Thirty feet long? However, it's a little longer than it is wide?"

George: "Oh, yeah, and there's a slit in the roof."

Emerson: "A slit in the roof?"

George: "Everything comes up to the centre and then there seems to be an opening down the middle."

Emerson: "But it's not a gabled roof but a rounded one?"

George: "Yeah, comes up and over like that. It's not a smooth slot, it's ragged. There was still about a two-foot slot down through the centre, and it's not square."

Paddy: "Is there smoke coming through the slot?"

George: "Yeah, but at the ends it's not. . .not cornered, it seems to be oval. Yeah, round ends, like a cigar. There are others like it around but they are a little bit off; they weren't laid one of them beside the other. There's one here—it's not that big a place, really. There's lots of places around where they seem to have the poles in at an angle. Together at the top for hanging stuff on."

Paddy: "That's racks for drying fish?"

George: "Yeah, that's what it seems to be."

Paddy: "Got the feeling there were lots of fish here."

George: "Well, I can't see too much of that. It seems to me there were lots of. . .there weren't that many people, you know. I wouldn't call it a huge place, not like some of them were. . .. Oh, I would say, right here, not more than 275 people at the very top, but there weren't that many all the time, understand? That was the maximum."

By this time George had carefully traced, in some detail, the outer walls of the house by walking around them. Paddy had stuck pins in the ground at George's suggestions. When the circuit was completed, Paddy mapped the location of the pins, set up a covering grid system and began to dig.

About six weeks and many, many wheelbarrows of dirt later, the excavation was completed. The house was revealed in all its detail, just where George had said it would be. Paddy felt that the recovery within the perimeter of the house of a nearly complete though broken ceramic vessel (a discovery which is quite rare) was a sort of bonus gift for his faith and his work. He announced himself, in any case, as impressed.

And I. . .I had the confused and confusing memory of Cahiague wiped quite out of my mind. I had felt that these sessions and those at Quackenbush were fairly impressive, even though ambiguous. But this! It seemed to me, from my vantage point as an archeologist of some experience in the field, that to do what George had just done by guesswork or luck was completely beyond the bounds of possibility.

He might have made a lucky hit on the palisade—though I doubt even that—but there is no way a guess could have followed the twists and turns and corners, nor hit on that peculiar gate. And there is, I am satisfied, no possibility that a guess would have found even a corner of that house, never mind the whole thing in all its detail. I was forced to accept George on his own terms.

No, either George had been there 15 or so years before (long enough to let the fields grow up again) with a large and skilled archaeological team with a large grant of money for the work and which had then carefully and systematically covered all evidence of its presence, or he was what he said he was: a man with real psychic abilities. I would, I assure you, rather have believed in this phantom archaeological team, but I could not. I was forced to accept George on his own terms.

Clearly, time for games was now over. This was the real thing.

I was in a state of some agitation by this point. Just as I had looked for evidence of chicanery or for some "natural" explanation for what George actually did, so I searched for a "natural" explanation for what "it"—this thing I had called intuition—was and how "it" "worked"—thereby plunging myself back into a thicket of quotation marks. I sought comfort in the still-mysterious realms of physics and chemistry, in energy theories and vibrations.

Maybe, I thought, all artifacts are "imprinted" with the life and energy and experience they have gained throughout their existence on earth.

This didn't tell me much, of course, though it might help explain why George is not always right; it must be as difficult to read this evidence as it is to decipher a foreign language in a strange alphabet. Maybe all artifacts are like self-contained storage-receiver sets; it would take a special sensitivity, like George's, to tap the output channels of such sets.

I was much comforted, in my early efforts to put skepticism to rest, to hear that a research physicist had devised a method whereby he could play Beethoven's Fifth Symphony to a properly-housed rock. After considerable exposure, the rock would obligingly play the Symphony back. Motivation aside (Physicists are mysterious people; why would he want a musical rock?) it does seem to suggest that there are storage mechanisms we don't fully comprehend.

I remember I once had the privilege (and it *was* a privilege) of watching the production of an obsidian tool by a very accomplished toolmaker. The demonstration was a fascinating combination of modern scientific knowledge and creativity. As the knapper sat in front of a group of students, he deftly chipped away at a block of obsidian using an assortment of bone tools.

He talked about fracture planes, hinge fractures, and a variety of technical geophysical matters well beyond my ken. He had great control of his material, removing flakes of just the right thickness, shape, and size to achieve the desired form. His bone tools delivered blows not too heavy, not too light—just right. His whole body worked as a unit with the tool being used and the artifact being produced.

The toolmaker explained that each tool was a special problem and a unique thing. Each new artifact was the result of a brain-computerization of all the experience he had gained in the production of previous artifacts. Tool production was not just a rational process, but was a total body experience—a combination of external and deep visceral clues.

The demonstration took the better part of an hour. When the man finished he was sweating. I asked, "You must be exhausted?"

He smiled. "I am. It *is* exhausting."

That demonstration came back to me vividly. "Yes," I thought, "it must be something like that—some form of imprinted energy storage we don't yet understand." If it were possible at all, I believe that man had "imprinted" himself on his tool.

But George's mysterious "informants" were altogether more up-setting. What was I to make of them? Maybe, I thought, maybe I can translate them, too, into concepts of energy. Maybe an "informant" is just the way George interpreted the data available to him. Another person would "see" them differently—as "forces," perhaps, or something else. . .If I could make them over from "spirits" into "residual free energy" or some such euphemism, it would be easier for my scientifically-trained mind to accept.

But as I went to sleep that night I thought, "Using language in this way is a psychological trick, a way of deceiving the mind into accepting the unacceptable, by indulging in gratuitous redefinition. It certainly doesn't get me any closer to understanding what 'it' is."

Chapter 7

Intuitive Archaeology:
The Argillite Carving
A Paper by Dr. Emerson

[The following paper was given by Dr. Emerson at Whitehorse Yukon, Northwest Territories, at the Canadian Archaeological Association meeting in March of 1974.]

This paper holds that intuitive or psychic knowledge stands as a viable alternative to the knowledge obtained by the more traditional methods of science.

In March 1973, I stated in a paper to the Canadian Archaeological Association that it was my conviction that I had received knowledge about archaeological artifacts and archaeological sites from a psychic informant, who related this information to me without any evidence of the conscious use of reasoning.[1] It was argued that learning, mind-reading and mental telepathy were not involved.

The most helpful evaluation of my paper was received from Dr. J.B. Rhine, founder of American parapsychology. Dr. Rhine has long been associated with Duke University and, although retired, is the very active director of the Foundation for Research Into the Nature of Man at Durham, North Carolina.

I quote:

> The value of this paper, in my judgment, depends upon what it does to the author, and those who hear or read it, in the way of further action. It has evidently led you to a decision to take seriously the possibility of a parapsychic function in George's performance. If it suffices for that, it has had an acceptable value. Conclusions and more important valuations can be left to the kind of thing you will be led to do by this paper. It is a pilot finding and that is one of the links in the chain of the search for truth.[2]

Upon hearing the 1973 paper, Mr. Jack Miller of Pt. Clements, B.C., was immediately stimulated to further action. He presented to me a black carved argillite stone artifact to be psychically studied. Mr. Miller did not reveal to us what he knew about the artifact. He secretly believed it represented a Sasquatch. Others had speculated that it was an unfinished pipe blank. The time and location of the find were known, but there was no significant archaeological context.

My psychic informant, George, when presented with the artifact at the annual banquet of the Canadian Archaeological Association, stated that it was carved by a Negro from Port Au Prince in the Caribbean. I, too, was moved to action. I was appalled. I was convinced that George was patently wrong; for to me as an archaeologist, the material was British Columbian black argillite. Any suggestion that it was carved by a black man from the Caribbean seemed to me to be the wildest flight of fancy. I suggested to George that the study be deferred until we returned home to Ontario.

After our return, George studied the carving further and presented me with an even more fantastic story, namely: the carver was a Negro born and raised in Africa. He was taken as a slave to the New World, where he worked in the Caribbean. He was later taken to British Columbia on an English ship; he escaped, met the natives, was accepted, married, lived, and died there. A fantastic story to me in April 1973, but not quite so fantastic in March 1974.

Then a series of strange things began to happen.

[Dr. Emerson's paper describes verbatim the series of readings by his daughter's roommate Sandy and his brother-in-law Jim that confirmed my reading of the carving (see Chapter 3).]

I was now stimulated to further positive action. The idea of a "psychic pool" to carry out comparative study of this artifact evolved. Independently, with no knowledge of what anyone else had said, and with no information about where it had been found or under what circumstances, it was given to seven additional intuitive or psychic persons for study. I stress that for each of them, confronted cold with the carving, it would have been easy to assume that it came from any place or any time in the world.

This study has occupied nearly a year; several hundred pages of transcribed, tape-recorded texts have been accumulated. Amazingly, the story related by George in April 1973 has been confirmed and reconfirmed by new members as they were added to the psychic team and they, in turn, have added information and confirmed each other's statements.

The material presented in this paper is only the briefest abstraction of the available texts and represents only the tip of an analytical iceberg. It seeks to document the feasibility and credibility of the "psychic team" approach and addresses itself to confirming three salient points:

1. The carver was from Africa.
2. He was brought to the New World as a slave.
3. He came to British Columbia.

On the topic of African origins, let us now consider excerpts from the tape-recorded statements of our psychic informants, Jim, George, Sandy, and Sheila:

Jim: "He came from Africa, as I said before, about half way down the west coast of Africa and about 30 miles inland. . ."

George: "There was a certain amount of water where he come from. . .there's waterfalls, quite high waterfalls. . .the central. . .west central, it seems to me. It was very heavy, very thick jungle. . .it was very heavy, very dense, very wet, very damp."

Sandy: "He was from the interior of North Africa. . .now there was a lot of French influence in North Africa, but he wasn't in that area, directly involved with the French. He was more in a jungle area going from the desert area into the savannah area of North Africa, savannah land."

Sheila: "Somebody who handled this at one time was a coloured man. . .the jungle is behind me here. . .It's not really jungle country, though. It's hot. I feel as though I'm up on a high plateau. . .high up, and the ocean is far down below. It is a very big plateau and a lot of dried grassland, lots of bush, and there are lots of trees, but you know, there is lots of space and grasslands in between the trees, so it is not jungle."

Jim states that the carver comes from Africa. George clearly describes the damp, wet jungle country. Sandy confirms the jungle environment but also sees savannah land. Sheila sees the jungle behind her but describes the dried grassland and brush of the savannah country before her. There can be little doubt that the psychics see the homeland of the carver located in northwest Africa, perhaps the Gold Coast area.

On the second point, that he was brought to the New World as a slave, we first hear from George.

> *George:* "I don't know whether he was picked up in a group or whether he was sold by other people. Anyway, he ended up in slavery; he came over in a slave ship."
>
> *Sandy:* "And he was a victim of a massive, sweeping slave trade insofar as people went into the interior because they needed men to come to the New World to work for them."
>
> *Jim:* "They were raided by a renegade African and his cohorts who captured quite a few of his village, including his own family, to sell them as slaves to the English or the Americans."

The psychic evidence that the carver was brought to the New World as a slave appears to be confirmed. For point three, that he came to British Columbia:

> *Jim:* "He made the carving out of the black rock from the mountains there nearby. . .in the west part of the North American continent. Canada comes to mind, but the United States has some connotations in here and so I can't say whether it is the American or Canadian side."
>
> *George:* "Anyway, he got on a boat and got over to the Pacific side. That was in B.C. that he did that. . .be around Bella Coola and Bella Bella, Bella Walla. . .up there in that area, that general direction up there, south of Prince Rupert."
>
> *Sheila:* "Kind of looks like the kind of stuff that comes from the Queen Charlotte Islands. . .what is a black man doing in the Queen Charlotte Islands?"

It is a good question. What is a black man doing in the Queen Charlotte Islands? But there seems little doubt about it in the minds of the psychics. With the whole world to choose from, Jim locates him in northwestern North America. George sees him in B.C. around Bella Coola, Bella Bella, and Prince Rupert. The artifact was found at Skidgate, on the Queen Charlotte Islands, which is located 200 miles northwest of Bella Coola and Bella Bella and 100 miles southwest of Prince Rupert, while Sheila actually sees the material as coming from the Queen Charlotte Islands. The artifact was found one-fourth of a mile south of Skidgate, Q.C.I.

On October 8, 1973, our psychic Sheila, in a state of deep trance, recorded a text for me which I found remarkable for its beauty, emotion, and clarity. It is sheer dramatic prose. To me it illustrates convincingly the great telepathic power of this argillite talisman.

> *Sheila:* ". . .and are we hungry, my brother and me. . .and we are waiting. . .and we sit and we watch. . .and I have in my belt a knife. . .and it chops and it cuts and it can cut out the spirit from the rock. From a tree. . .but only that spirit that which is given to be taken out. . .and I think that knife could cut the spirit from a man.
>
> ". . .and we take from the bank a rock that sticks forth, and my brother and I take much rock. . .much rock. . .flat, like. . .like a sheet. . .I see in the rock a face, and I see other spirit faces, and they show to me that they must be taken from the rock. . .and I cut, and I cut. My brother, he cuts. . .and we make a ship. . .we see the spirit of the ship; and my brother cuts a ship, but I. . .I cut the spirit of the baba and I see the spirit of. . .
>
> ". . .Kajah. . .Kajah. . .Kajah, she who was left and my son. . .my son. . .we cut and we shape, and the spirit comes to us from the rock. . .and my brother sees the spirit of the ship in the wood, for there is a large wood. . .oh, a branch, on the beach, and he fashioned this ship from the branch. . .and we forget our hunger, for we are big men.
>
> ". . .and I see my hand. . .I hold it before my face; I feel the wind blow from the sea through my hand. . .and I see the fingers. . .long. . .my hand. . .long. . .I see the bones sticking forth, I see my arm. . .long. . .bone thin.
>
> ". . .I, and my brother, are hungry. . .but the hunger of our bellies is not like the hunger of the spirit. . .and of our hearts. . .Kajah. . ."

As I mentioned, the material presented is only a tip of an iceberg of information. However, it does seem patently evident that at least three statements about this artifact are psychically confirmed.

The carver was born and raised in Africa.

He was brought to the New World as a slave.

He did come to British Columbia.

I am now convinced that it can be argued that intuitive or psychic knowledge does stand as a viable alternative to knowledge obtained by the more traditional science. by utilizing a psychic team, and by cross analysis of their independent statements which reveal an amazing degree of correspondence and concurrence, I am convinced that we have been able to abstract intuitive truth about at least one man's past. In the study of this one item, we have gone far beyond the limits of chance and coincidence as an explanation.

In my previous paper, I stated that "by means of the intuitive and the parapsychological, a whole new vista of man and his past stands ready to be grasped." By this kind of research I have been able to recover three major events in the life of this obscure African carver. The text available will allow me to recover much more, with a wealth of detail about this man who has otherwise been unknown or obscured in traditional history. If the life of this black man is available, why not the life of all men? As it has been said, "By their works ye shall know them." It is a mind-boggling thought.

I do not wish to convey the idea that I am so enamoured of the psychic or the psychic pool that I am prepared to ignore the findings and resources of traditional science. Rather, I consider that progress will only be made by a moulding and an integration of the two—intuition and science.

At this point, I offer an illustration. On April 25, 1973, I was fortunate to obtain the following diagnosis of the argillite carving from Mr. Allen Tyyska, a graduate anthropologist who, because of his experience as a cataloguer of African art specimens at the Royal Ontario Museum, was well-equipped to provide the following statement for me:

Allen: "While I was cataloguing at the Royal Ontario Museum, we had a large collection come in from West Africa. Mr. Mayfield, who lives just west of Toronto, goes on trips and he bought things. And, well, there was a large number of sculptures and little passport masks and things that all came from the upper Volta, the Niger, and generally that area of west Africa between Sierra Leone and the Cameroon, along that coast, you know, Nigeria, Gold Coast, Ghana. . ."

Emerson: "I was going to say, that is what they call the Gold Coast."

Allen: "Yeah. So this little piece of argillite looks like it fits into those art styles, and there are a number of things about it that would belong in that general area. . .maybe more precisely along the upper reaches of the Volta. Like. . .you see how thin it is, relative to how long it is. That's a pretty good characteristic of that art style. . .When you look at the face. . .just the face on its own. . .you see that it's got. . .like. . .that nose is sort of triangular in its section there.

That's the way they used to break the face down into planes, on the passport masks of the Dan. For example, the face would be a series of planes. . .geometric planes that came together to block out the features; and this is about the way they did it. . .that deep notch below the eyes. . .sort of the way that eyebrow is one of a kind plane and there is a notch below it for the mouth. And this chin being in a different plane. . .that little groove above the eyebrows. . .all those things are just in that art style."

Mr. Tyyska felt that the art styles manifest to him by the carving are to be found specifically in the Gold Coast area of West Africa and, perhaps more precisely, "the upper reaches of the Volta."

This certainly appears to coincide with the statements of our psychic informants, although environmental statements need to be checked out in detail. But it has been encouraging and salutary to have the ideas of the psychics apparently confirmed by evidence drawn from a knowledge of African art.

In a similar vein, I am well aware that there is a host of topics which can be abstracted from the text material which can be tested by the accumulated knowledge of anthropology, ethnology, ethnohistory, geology, history, musicology, primatology, and a wide variety of other sciences.

George has given me detailed information upon native behaviour that can only be the "potlatch." Sandy has given me information on how the carver produced the throwing element in the Spanish or Mexican Jai Alai game. Sheila gave me the name of a ship to be searched out. She gave me a detailed description of the British Columbia shoreline where the carver and his brother were.

Maureen, George, and Sheila were conscious of the presence of Russian sailing ships and Sheila described them. We know they were along the coast at that time harvesting sea otters. George said that the carver came to British Columbia on an English sailing ship, and Maureen wondered why she could hear old English sea chanteys being sung. Tom, in both word and by body movements, provided me with me with a description of a native African dance.

Sheila heard the shrieks of monkeys and baboons swishing through the trees just as the sun went down. Is this typical primate behaviour? These are all questions to be studied and researched. Such a program could lead to the integration of intuition and scientific knowledge.

I assure you that I approached these studies with an open-minded skepticism. The fantastic story which George told me in April 1973 I now find not so fantastic in March 1974.

I offer in conclusion another statement from our psychic, Sandy: "The individual I see as being reddish-yellow-red. . .red. . .red-brown. . .big, hairy. . .because I keep getting this picture of this ape-man going about his business."

And so there it is: reddish, red-brown, big, hairy—an ape man going about his business. Doesn't it sound rather like the legendary descriptions of the Sasquatch? Mr. Jack Miller seems to have been vindicated and perhaps rewarded for the day that he handed his argillite carving to George and me for intuitive study. Or, in the words of the editor of the *Queen Charlotte Observer*: "So. . .although authorities may yet make a gorilla out. . .of a Sasquatch, they'll never make a monkey out of Jack Miller of Port Clements, Q.C.I."

References:

[1]*The Midden*, Publication of the Archaeological Society of British Columbia, Vol. V. No. 3, June, 1973, pp. 16-20.

[2]Personal Communication from Dr. J.B. Rhine, August 6, 1973.

Chapter 8

Comments by George

Dr. Emerson had handed me the argillite carving during the banquet after the final meeting in Vancouver of the Canadian Archaeological Association. I was rather tired and feeling the effects of a heavy meal. The people around were, it seems, all talking at once, but I tried to concentrate as well as I could on the carving. All I could really get was that it was carved by a black man. When I told Dr. Emerson this, he had an incredulous look on his face. I wondered if it had been a mistake.

Later, I returned to my motel room, and for the next few days I thought about this and still got the same answer in respect to the carving being done by a black man. I began to get more details as I meditated on the argillite carving; so when I again met Norm, I knew the full story, incredible as it was. When I reconfirmed what I had said to him at Vancouver and told him the rest of the story, Norm was silent for a long time.

Then, with his usual good humour, he laughed and said this is so unbelievable he would have to think about it for awhile. Well, for a whole year he worked on this with other psychics, and he ended up with the same story. Somehow, I still believe he had reservations in his mind, even when he presented the paper, because this was not a science that he could relate to with his knowledge and background. I can understand and sympathize with his inner turmoil. It was even a fantastic story to me, although I knew it to be true. No one who heard the story about the argillite carving said it was not possible. But then again, not many said it was probable, either.

Chapter 9

The Gorilla Argillite

From Dr. Emerson's Papers: An Outsider's Account

[Among Dr. Emerson's papers was this manuscript in third person on the argillite carving. Ann tells me that an older man who was a part-time reporter consulted a number of times with Norman, read his many pages of research, listened to the tapes, and wrote this paper intending to submit it to a newspaper or journal. But in the end he decided against it (perhaps because his health was rapidly failing; he died shortly afterwards) and gave the paper to Dr. Emerson to use as he saw fit.

Norman had intended using it in the book which he started and did not ever manage to finish. It gives a different perspective from an outsider's point of view on the work. The paper follows.]

The thing is black. Not the glittering black of coal, but the deep translucent black of a night sky in summer—the colour, perhaps, of a man born and raised on the far reaches of the African Upper Volta. It is made of stone. Not rough-textured granite, nor flaky gneiss, but something smooth and warm to the touch. It is flat on two sides, about as thick as a man's finger. It is irregularly shaped, seemingly without design or purpose.

But on the leading edge there is carved a face—appearing to have been done with a few quick, skillful slashes with the carver's chisel, done with a cartoonist's skill in broad strokes. Character had been carved with just a few lines—here a slash, showing strength. There a slash, denoting power. Here a cut, deepening the enigma. There are a few more sharp angles to refine character and the face emerges: squat, powerful, with just a hint of brutality in it—a thing to be treated carefully, with reverence perhaps, or with admiration.

It sits easily in the palm. There is a curiously greasy warmth to the stone. It is very tactile. There is no coldness to it. It feels heavy, solid, confident. There is no timidity to it, either. It feels—important. It doesn't feel like the kind of piece a whittler would do in an idle moment and then casually toss aside. Those who have handled it have felt this.

It is, in archaeological terms, an artifact. But this, of course, tells you nothing. Obviously it is an artifact; some artisan, somewhere, sometime made it. The riddle (and it is riddles that keep the archaeologists fascinated; it is a profession that attracts jigsaw puzzlers and detectives) is, who made it? Where? And when? Why was it made? How did it come to be discarded on the Queen Charlotte Islands off the British Columbia Coast? What was he doing there in the first place? What was the purpose or use of the artifact?

Archaeology is a science of detection. It has built up over the years a formidable array of detection techniques, ranging from detailed cross-referencing to the sophisticated analysis of the radioactive isotope carbon-14 used for dating purposes. Detailed pictures of certain vanished cultures have been built up by analyzing the artifacts they have left behind.

Some astonishingly informative pictures have emerged. Of course, archaeology cannot provide the richness of texture and corroborating detail of conventional history; it can only guess at the psychology and sociology of a lost society.

Occasionally also, an artifact is found where the "archaeological context"—the supportive circumstantial detail—is not available. Sometimes artifacts just don't seem to fit the cultures that inhabited the places where they were found; just as geologists often find boulders they call "erratics," which don't bear any relationship to other rock types in the neighbourhood, so archaeologists find "erratic" artifacts. Usually they are tagged and put away to await further evidence.

This black stone carving is such an artifact. It is made of argillite, a slate-like stone, sometimes soft as wood, native to the Queen Charlotte Islands. Indians of the region used argillite a lot for their carving. But they carved nothing like this. Nothing at all.

Jack Miller, an enthusiastic amateur archaeologist who lives in Port Clements, Queen Charlotte Islands, was the man who found the carving. He was with Dr. Knut Fladmark of Simon Fraser University when the carving was discovered in the course of digging a post hole on the property of Arnold and Pearl Pearson, a quarter-mile south of Skidgate, Q.C.I.

Before the Pearsons bought the property it was, rather unromantically, the site of The Dogfish Liver Rendering Plant. Before that, there was a lodge there owned by a mysterious person known locally as "The Captain." The site's history before "The Captain" is unknown.

Miller, who referred to the carving as "the gorilla argillite," was fascinated by it, without knowing what it was. He secretly believed it might represent an anonymous Indian's attempt to render the Sasquatch—the legendary reddish-brown, hairy, man-like beast of the Pacific Coast (known in the United States as Bigfoot), but he had no proof of this. All he knew was where it was found and when. There was no further data; no one knew who had carved it or discarded or lost it, or had any idea when.

It was at this point that Miller and Emerson met at the annual meeting of the Canadian Archaeological Association. Emerson had just delivered the meeting's most controversial paper on a new field of research he called "intuitive archaeology," and Miller was interested. He resolved to pass the argillite carving to Emerson for further study.

He did so that evening at the annual banquet of the Association held in a Vancouver hotel. Emerson gave it to George, his psychic informant, who was sitting at the same table. George—or so Emerson thought at the time—blew it.

He held the carving in his hand for study, as is his habit when "psychometrizing" (investigating through psychic means) an artifact. He had been given no data on the carving at all; as far as he was concerned it might have come from Pago Pago, or New Guinea, or New York City.

After a time he announced that it wasn't done by an Indian at all, but by a black man from the Caribbean—more specifically Port au Prince. Emerson was appalled. He was convinced that George was hopelessly wrong, for he knew the material was argillite, native to B.C., and this whole thing about a black man from the Caribbean seemed like the wildest flight of fancy. Yet he knew by this time some of the hazards of psychic detection, and also some of the difficulties faced by his informants. In this case, George was sitting at a table with a number of skeptical people, and there were one or two people there he actively disliked.

Norman knew this could affect George's performance. After all, psychometry is a delicate and sensitive use of little-understood mental abilities, and it was not surprising that emotional states would have some effect on its outcome. Psychometry is not an exact science in the sense mathematics is; there are too many variables and too many ways of affecting both data and performance. So, while appalled at the outcome of the "test," he suggested to George that they put off further study of the carving until later. George agreed. Miller was willing to lend the carving for study.

Back in George's home near Peterborough, Ontario, and again at Emerson's rural home outside Toronto, George further studied the carving. He held it, studied it, fondled it, extracting from it all he could. He came up with a story even more unbelievable than the first—though it was not a contradiction but an elaboration.

The carver, George said, was indeed a black man. He was born and raised in Africa and was taken to the New World as a slave, where he worked for a while in the Caribbean area. He was at this time with Spanish-speaking people. He was later taken to British Columbia on an English ship—George did not trace the details of this change of fortune. The carver had escaped, met the natives, been accepted, married, had children, lived, and died there.

He carved, George felt, because he was from a carving tradition; he worked in stone rather than his more familiar material, wood, because it was the local custom and he wanted to prove to his adopted people that he wasn't going to be the local equivalent of a welfare bum—that he could contribute something positive to their society, and not simply be a drain on it.

Stroking the carving, George sketched in what details he could. The date—the time sequence—was always hard to guess at, partly because his informants didn't themselves know, and did not use the same calendar as we do.

George: ". . .he came to this country, it seems to me, around 16. . .well, 1690 to 1720, between there. . .he was taken a slave, but had quite a career. He was working with the Jesuits to start with, helping establish the sugar cane plantation that they had down there [Port au Prince, Haiti].

"Anyway, he got on a boat and got over to the Pacific somehow—something to do with fishing. . ."

Emerson: "You told me he jumped off the ship and swam ashore?"

George: "That was up in B.C. he did that. . .It was in what we would call the Straits. . .or the northern part of that, up at the top of it somewhere."

Emerson: "Was it on the mainland?"

George: "Well, he was on the island and on the mainland; he was on both. He did a lot of fishing while he was there, Norm. When he was with these people he did a lot of fishing.

He was pretty good on the water; it was second nature to him, he came from water country. . ."

Emerson: "You told me he came from Africa, right? You pinned that down last time?"

George: "There was a certain amount of water where he came from. . .There was definitely a big river, a very rough place, see. . .he knew the crocodile, he knew the snakes, he was quite at home on it, he had been around water when he was at home as a boy. He was swimming then but he wasn't completely. . .he was no savage.

"He had a little finesse about him—his people had finesse about them. . .I can see him collecting, it looks like a fruit of some kind and it's not a banana, but is a. . .anyway this stuff was dried and pounded into a flour—you could call it a fruit or a vegetable. He collected this stuff. But mostly just hunting. He did a lot of fishing there, too. There's very heavy forest there and he was quite familiar to the gorilla. . ."

Emerson: "He was quite familiar with the gorilla?"

George: "Oh, very, yeah. Such thick forest. It was very damp. They didn't see the sky too much. When they were around where the gorilla was they couldn't see the sky. It was very heavy, very dense, very wet, very damp. They didn't inhabit that place all the time, though. Not themselves.

"I don't know whether he was picked up in a group or was sold by other people. Anyway, he ended up on a slave ship and it was the Spanish who brought him over here—the Spanish and the Portuguese. Portuguese and Spanish people both. . .and he was fortunate or unfortunate in coming up to the Spanish part; and it was certainly on the west coast of Africa where he was shipped out."

Emerson: "How did he get to B.C.? On a Spanish ship?"

George: "No, it was an English ship. They were all English-speaking and not that bad a people. They wore very coarse clothes, there was nothing in the sense that they were soldiers. They wore a funny, coarse dress. Their boat was certainly not the best."

Emerson: "Were they up there fishing, or exploring?"

George: "Both, they were fishing and exploring and they were what you would call. . .They weren't the nicest people, you know, they wouldn't hesitate to steal anything they could lay their hands on. They were up there to take what they could get."

Emerson: "Now, you told me when he jumped ship he

spent time in a swamp area?"

George: "Yeah, very wet, mouth of the river, lots of rivers, very cold—he wasn't too used to this kind of cold dampness. Probably it was the time of year as the weather improved while he was there. It was probably in the early spring when he did jump. He had to make out on his own, you know."

As Emerson has said, a fantastic story, seemingly without basis in fact; yet George seemed so sure. As he often did when psychometrizing, the information would be extracted in bits, in dribbles, the later pieces occasionally contradicting the earlier statements as George became more sure of the picture. Emerson has since learned not to worry about these seeming contradictions; he has found that the earlier information is usually vague and the later statements almost always more reliable. In this case, there was some contradiction, but very little. George seemed so certain.

The problem for an archaeologist and a scientist was that George's story, which seemed so wildly off-base, was inherently uncheckable. It seemed, then, that there was no way the story could be verified. Sure, circumstantially it was barely possible; there were slave traders, there were explorers—Russian, English, Spanish, and Portuguese—up and down the Pacific coast. The argillite carving did seem, superficially, African-looking. But all this fanciful stuff about jungles! Gorillas! English sailors in homespun cloth! There was no handle there to grasp; no one hard piece of verifiable information which could either substantiate, or disprove the story. . .

Or was there?

By this time Emerson had been working with George for some time and had come to sense when George was sure and when he was not. He had come to trust his assessments, too; those that could be checked out did so with often more than an 80-percent accuracy. . .

When Ann had asked George if he had been aware of the Sasquatch when he was doing the reading, he told her oh, yes. It was when the carver and the natives had sighted one that the black man had felt free to carve a representation of the gorilla he had known in his youth.

This black man looked, and was, so different from the natives that he had to be very careful what he said or did in order to be acceptable, as he had no other real choice. He needed to be with them to survive and have a life.

Events then happened that brought two other psychic people into Norman's life; and when given the carving they came up with stories similar to George's. Emerson was pleased. He hit upon the idea of a "psychic pool."

Through chance and the circles Ann was associating with, a number of people with psychic abilities were introduced into Norman's life just as he needed them. In all, seven different sensitives were given the carving to "read." Not all were as able to intuit the whole scenario, but each in his own way sensed the same outline and added something credible to the story.

The comparison of this material was the subject of Emerson's second paper, also given at the annual meeting of the C.A.A. This time there were almost no questions asked and he was elected president of the C.A.A. It seemed that intuitive archaeology was being accepted into Canadian professional circles.

One of the popular misconceptions about psychics is that they need to operate in darkened rooms, murkily lit, to obtain their information—presumably so the "spirits" on the "other side" won't be harmed by the light. Emerson's information was obtained from his psychics in much more routine and mundane ways—sitting in his sunny living room, overlooking a meadow with its winding creek. Only once have they held what is regarded as a genuine "seance" and that time it didn't really work (partly, perhaps, because the chemistry and motives of the individuals involved clashed).

Only rarely do psychics feel the need to go into trance, and when they do so, it is often quickly, without warning and without any props or stage management. In this state, sometimes most interesting and human material is garnered, as when Sheila brought through the haunting aside about "Kajah."

George does not go into trance. And it is in George's tapes that the truly mind-boggling nature of what Emerson's research is bringing out becomes apparent. If there is anything to it, the wealth of material he has been able to gather from just this one obscure African, otherwise unknown to history, opens up completely new areas for the study of mankind. George has occasionally fumbled on certain aspects. Certain things he cannot "see" or recover. There are gaps in the "memory" he has access to. But he is able to provide fascinating insights into the psychology of lost peoples which conventional archaeology could never extrapolate.

Who the carver was, we cannot know. But what he was like and how he believed, we can. Listen again to George:

George: "Yeah, they [the B.C. Indians] accepted him. He became part of them, became a brother to them. He had children, he lived there and was part of their society. He added a lot to them. As I told you before, they were such. . .superstitious people, they damn near came to where it was impossible for them to live."

Emerson: "You told me they had a lot of ceremonies that went on?"

George: "Oh gawd yes, every day was a ceremony. Getting up in the morning to breathe the first breath of air was a ceremony. Everything was the spirit of something or the spirit of something else—so damn many spirits there. Jeez, the grass, the trees, the leaves, the wind, the clouds, the water, the fish, the birds—everything had a spirit. Each one of them meant something and it got so bad and they were so superstitious that they practically ceased to exist for a long time due to this, and it got to be real *stupid,* you know, and they couldn't do anything unless they first had to appease this spirit or that spirit. . ."

Emerson: "You told me quite a bit about how these people worked and one thing or another—do you recall that?"

George: "Well, their mainstay right around there was fishing, generally the fishing. They took great amounts of fish. No problem getting it. They were quite good in the water, quite good at seamanship. The type of equipment they had— the canoes—were quite good-sized boats that were quite seaworthy. All during the centuries they had lots of visitors, Norm, from other places."

Emerson: "You mentioned that the English in that ship were not the first white men they had seen."

George: "That was the north end of the island—the big island. They knew the white men had come there, some English-speaking white men, they had seen them before. They had seen other white men who were talking with a different dialect, and they. . .well, I know they were Russians, though they didn't know that. They were Russian-speaking people, these—the flat Slovak-type faces, you know. This fellow came along quite a bit after.

"But a long time before white men ever came, other people came from different places from across the ocean in a different type of boat. In fact, these people copied their final design that they had from boats that came there from other places, and boats even drifted in. They drifted in to their shores and they copied them. There's lots of these they couldn't understand. They got material they couldn't understand what it

was. . .They had no way of making it, you know. They had
a cloth that came in there, they had no idea what kind of
cloth it was."

Emerson: "Did they make cloth themselves, do you know?"

George: "Yeah, they had a cloth—a rough, coarse cloth—
vegetable, I would say. They put more work into it and it
was a little bit more. . .ugh. . .better done than the cloth they
made here [Ontario] from the birch or the cedar that the
Indians around here made. It's hard to understand it. They
weren't pressed to survive, like they were here where we
are. They had more chance for the cultural side of life, for
improving their lot or their life than they had here because
of the game, fish, and fruit and no real enemies because of
the mountains. . ."

Emerson: "They had cloth. Do you get any idea of these
including blankets?"

George: "Yeah, they had blankets. They definitely had a
blanket, oh yes. They had cloth and they could cover themselves, too. Not in the sense that it was a beautiful piece of
work—nothing like that, really. They did do some painting
on ceremonial objects. Very little in the sense that, they felt,
they were lucky to have it, never mind decorating it. The
fact that they had it was decoration enough. Oh, gee, I don't
know, some stuff. . .like things they could do. . .oh, I don't
know, it appears to me. . .they could do really good things
with the skins of fish, a real big fish, they could do things
with the skins of that fish. They made it pretty much like a
cloth. They even had skin that they used to polish
things. . .They did so many things!"

Emerson: "Do you get a picture of what kind of houses
they lived in?"

George: "Depending on where they were. Some were just
a rough lean-to affair, a lean-to roof. Some were conical,
higher in the centre and circular. . .They seem to be higher
in the centre and slope out. For shedding water. They had a
certain number of these."

Emerson: "Did they ever destroy things, George? We realize they gave things away. Do you ever get any picture of
them destroying things?"

George: "No, no—that would be a bad thing to destroy
something. . .because that thing had a spirit. Even when they
caught a fish, it's a heck of a thing to turn around and eat
that fish."

Emerson: "Do you get anything, a picture of big ceremonial things that today we call coppers?"

George: "Nothing comes. Coppers? I don't know what 'coppers' is."

Emerson: "Like a big sheet of copper plate? They didn't come into the picture here, probably."

George: "No, they did have copper."

Emerson: "Well, that's okay."

George: "But. . .they did look in the water and saw somebody else in there. They thought that was another world in there, that was the spirit world—that wasn't them. In calm water on a calm day they could go to the water and look at these other people down there, that was fantastic. And they had polished copper up so they could see these people. They thought that was great. They didn't recognize that as themselves, you know."

Emerson: "Is there any picture that they had any slaves?"

George: "Well, no, they didn't have slaves in that sense, no Indian had slaves in the sense of slaves like the white man had slaves. He had a choice, very similar to what Christians used to give you—you were going to be sacrificed to somebody, heh heh, you know, but if you chose to join them you were quite accepted by the tribe, you became just as important in the tribe as anyone else."

Emerson: "That Negro chap who came, he was very definitely like a blood brother, eh?"

George: "Right, he was a brother."

Emerson: "Now, he did this carving and I think you gave me quite a bit of detail, how it looked like an ape, and you drew me the picture of the body that went with the head, and so on. Did he learn his carving when he was there?"

George: "No, no."

Emerson: "He knew how to carve?"

George: "He knew how to carve; he carved many things, not just this. This is from his childhood. But the things he carved were fish and not the walrus, he didn't see the walrus."

Emerson: "We don't really get any idea what he was trying to demonstrate when he carved that, or do we?"

George: "He was trying to tell them. . ."

Emerson: "What a gorilla was like?"

George: "Yeah, show them what he and his people worshipped. They held the gorilla in great reverence. They didn't kill him. They. . .he. . .the gorilla to them represented a nice homeland, the family, that sort of thing. There's other animals, too, that he carved for them he would show, and of course they didn't believe him; they didn't always believe him. But he brought to them a lot of medicine, too, you know; he was pretty good. He didn't get up to be what you would consider a 'witch doctor.' He never could be. They didn't trust him that much, carving things with heads like that."

Emerson: "You probably wouldn't know, but was that lost around where he lived?"

George: "No, it was taken away from where he lived with a lot of other stuff, too—a lot of other stuff taken, too, because when he died his family separated and they were great movers, they didn't stick around too long in one spot. They didn't, you know. If they needed to go down the coast a hundred miles, they didn't hesitate to."

Emerson: "They lived mainly on the coast?"

George: "Yeah, they lived on the coast. They didn't get in too far. They got the deer and I guess the moose. . ."

Emerson: "Did they have a lot of totem poles around their village?"

George: "They did, but it wasn't really *in* the village. They were put there to keep the bad ones out, you know."

Emerson: "These spirits we've been talking about?"

George: "Yeah, right. They're kept out there now, a lot of good ones are just put right out on the beach right down in the sand—little ones about that high—they looked to be about five feet high, and they're pushed down in the sand facing the water and some facing each direction. They all meant something to them: good fishing, poor fishing, keep that north wind out of us, away from us, keep the water from coming in from the ocean on us. . .They certainly wanted the snow to stay on the mountains, so they would pray to the mountain spirits there to keep that white stuff up there with them. They didn't want it down where they were. Made things a little difficult, you know, just as it would be for anybody else. But they had everything they wanted to do, these here, he made quite a few carvings on that line, this here isn't one of his best."

Emerson: "No?"

George: "In fact, it's rather a rough effort in comparison to some of the good stuff he did. He made several carvings of fish, you know, but they were used for other purposes, too, you know, and some were handles—various tools, he was very good at that. He did well."

Emerson: "He carved wood too?"

George: "Oh, yeah, he carved wood. He taught them a lot of things. A few of their faces came from him on their totem poles. Because he did some, you know, because he was good. Not everybody could do it, you know. But it's just like. . .being he was a stranger in another country, he had to adapt to their ways whether he agreed with them or not, you know."

Emerson: "The carving was one way he could do it?"

George: "Right."

Emerson: "They'd think that was great."

George: "They thought the person could make stories in stone or wood, you know. But then he was more desirous of staying there than of going back where he was before. He didn't want to go back to that kind of life, you know."

It is a rich brew that George has brought us and it matches, pretty well, the archaeological content—what is known of the artifact and the society of the west coast through traditional scientific means. This is, of course, Emerson's purpose, precisely—not to abandon findings and resources of traditional science, but to supplement them, to arrive at some new synthesis whereby intuition may give flesh to the scientific bones.

Emerson wants to use the psychic material to *add* to the traditional: here, with this artifact, he has the first experiment. If he is right, it calls for a new kind of science. It calls for a synthesis of the old and the new. It calls for a new kind of openness, of receptivity. Anthropologists and archaeologists, quite properly, are the kind of people who continually chip away at the potsherds of truth rather than make giant leaps of faith toward unknown goals. Those careful skills will always be needed and retained.

Emerson wants to involve also the hard disciplines of physics and biology in his new directions; wherever light can be shed and by whatever means, he wants to shed it. Hopefully, history will one day be able to incorporate some of the techniques now reserved for the writer of fiction or the spinner of fanciful tales—going beyond mere physical description to the interior monologue; from a description of the landscape to an exploration of the passions and emotions of some of the men and women who have been lost to history.

George's initial unbelievable story grows more secure the more research is done. Emerson, ever ready for his experience to be confounded and to have his theories challenged, willingly turned the argillite carving and a tape recorder and tapes over to a skeptical graduate student who said that any truck driver could think up a wild story like that. But the student was able to glean almost no stories and the ones he did gather were mundane and conflicting. This use of a "control group" suggests that George indeed was right and the skeptics were wrong.

There was one other interesting piece of information that came along later. Jack Miller wrote that he had learned there were records in the Provincial Court House in Victoria that indicated that some of the early Indians of that area had Negro characteristics.

In relation to the comments George made about the people who had visited in olden times and about the boats they copied from the ones that had drifted in and the strange cloth that they could not comprehend, a note could be made here. Thor Heyerdahl, who has studied tides, ocean currents, and ancient movements of peoples and their means of transportation, found much evidence that the coastal stream from Asia to the Americas drifted to the northern coast of the continent. That ancient peoples went with these currents and then made their way south along the coast.

Heyerdahl proved some of his beliefs by recreating the ships and rafts that he believed had been used in making these early voyages and by actually sailing their routes successfully. His research could well explain George's reference to the long-ago peoples who had visited this tribe and the materials that drifted in that puzzled them or the functional and seaworthy designs that they had copied from other peoples and these drifting boats.

Chapter 10

Intuitive Archaeology:
A Developing Approach
A Paper by Dr. Emerson

*[The third paper given by Dr. Emerson was at the annual meeting
of the American Anthropological Association in Mexico City, Mexico,
in November 1974. The world-famous anthropologist, Margaret Mead,
had persuaded the A.A.A. that parapsychology was a legitimate study
for anthropology, since it is the study of man, and they had added a
symposium on the subject to their annual meeting. Norman felt that
this step should be supported, and so he traveled there to give a
report on his research up until that time. He gave the following paper.]*

My research began on the level of fun and games when I learned
that my friend, George McMullen, could "psychometrize" artifacts;
that is, he could hold an object in his hand, concentrate upon it,
and then relate details about its history and the circumstances surrounding that object. When I found that he was giving me accurate
information, it took no major flash of insight for me to realize that
I had hundreds of excavated artifacts that could well benefit from
psychometry. George and I began to work.

I was understandably skeptical. However, George's "readings"
proved to be relevant and rich in detail. I was able to assess his
statements on the basis of knowledge of the sites I had excavated
and on a broad understanding of the archaeology, ethnohistory,
and history of the Ontario Iroquois people.

I next learned that George was psychometrically sensitive to
archaeological sites. We visited several. George would walk very
rapidly over the area to "orient" himself. Then he would tell me
about it. He would assess the age of the site, describe the people,
their dress, their dwellings, economy, and general behaviour. He
would also provide me with specific guidance. He indicated the
exact location of a palisade wall.

In one case he walked around the perimeter of an Iroquois longhouse which he could see but I could not, while I followed behind placing surveyor's pins in the ground. Six weeks later, the entire house was excavated exactly where he had said it would be. George's performance was thus testable not only by archaeological knowledge and ethnological data, but by follow-up excavation as well. I have estimated that George is 80-percent accurate.

The fact that human beings do have such abilities would seem to be demonstrated beyond a reasonable doubt. Persons such as Girard Crosiet, Peter Hurkos, and Olaf Johnson have been studied and reported in considerable detail. The readings of the late Edgar Cayce, the "Sleeping Prophet," have been intensively assessed and studied. As has been said by Stanley Krippner, "It is fairly easy to take isolated bits and pieces of the phenomena of life and sweep them under the rug year after year. But they start to accumulate and the bumps get enormous—you can't ignore them any more."

There is little consistent evidence known to me that archaeologists have employed intuitive or psychic persons in their excavation programs. The archaeological investigation of Glastonbury Abbey by Frederick Bligh Bond is perhaps a tragic precedent. Dr. Hans Holzer recorded a number of readings upon New and Old World sites by the English psychic, Dame Sibyl Leek. But these do not seem to have been followed up by any excavation program.

Professor Robert Redford of Lewis and Clark Community College in Illinois has recently been reported as being presented with evidence of a middle Mississippi culture from the psychometry of a human tooth by a psychic team. Other investigations are under way, but to attempt to discuss them here would be premature.

It is my impression that many field archaeologists, including myself, have had brushes with the psychic during their field investigations, but they have preferred to leave them, if not undiscussed, at least unpublished; and do not seem to have seen fit to follow them up in any way. Thus, there is little evidence for a convincing effort to develop a methodology involving the alliance of archaeology and parapsychology.

The monumental literature being produced on allied and relevant subjects cannot be ignored in research design. To date, my own studies have allowed me little time or energy to try to understand the operating process, or to seek answers to *why* it happens. My efforts have been mainly directed toward recording and carrying out no more than a beginning assessment of such reading.

In the search for explanations, a paraphysical answer would have great appeal and would suggest that the process is a "right-brain" function, and thus a human faculty. Yet, when the phenomenon is observed, it becomes increasingly difficult to ascribe psychic readings to a biophysical, or even a physio-psychological explanation.

To attribute such insights to "another personality," to the subconscious, or to the unconscious, does not provide a satisfactory answer nor does racial memory or the group unconscious. The possibility of spirit forces must be faced. The subject matter revealed is often so alien in time, space, and culture that a non-spiritual explanation leaves too many questions unanswered.

The data sources appear to follow a hierarchy of increased complexity from such phenomena as the Ouija board and automatic writing to dowsing and divination, through psychometry, meditation, hypnosis, telepathy, astral travel, and ultimately to trance mediumship. The function of intuition appears to occupy a somewhat neutral ground. It lies somewhere between science and spiritualism, between the rational truth of science and the revealed truth of revelation; between the hard-core natural sciences and esoteric science; between men and the gods. To me, it at least represents a researchable ground. In what direction such research will lead, I find it almost impossible to comprehend.

I do not see that the answers will lie in current orthodox science; nor am I yet prepared to leap forward into the realm of spirit guides, masters, and even more elevated galactic beings.

In the archaeological field and in allied parapsychological areas, the study of known energies and energy fields may provide clues. The study of magnetism and magnetic anomalies is promising. Little-known or virtually new energy sources call for study.

The accumulating evidence in favour of not only new kinds and sources of energy, but also for new possible levels of consciousness and new kinds of reality to be perceived, cannot be overlooked. This kind of thing we have done as anthropologists for many decades. Perhaps the greatest necessary step forward will be to restore the faith of scientists in such investigations so that such answers may be forthcoming. The role of faith in science is a matter often overlooked and underestimated.

It appears inevitable that redefinition of *science* and its scope must evolve and is already beginning. At the same time, a similar redefinition of *religion* must take place. The orthodoxies of each become more restrictive and less tenable day by day. A new fusion might lead to great discoveries. I am not sure that I am, nor is humanity, ready for such revisions any more than were those men who had to admit that the flat world was really round.

But the signs are increasingly all around us; the new days are urgently and restlessly on the horizon. There is an atmosphere of inevitability. It could be argued, as it has often been predicted for homo sapiens, that we are seeing the next step in the evolution of our particular form of man as the Aquarian Age unfolds.

Finally, I would suggest that no one enter into such studies lightly or facetiously. It is inevitable that one will be subject to a series of deep, profound, personal shocks. . .some pleasant, some unpleasant. One must become accustomed to the realization that, in terms of Jung's "synchronicity" and "meaningful coincidences," a pattern emerges which suggests that the research program is being "led" or "directed." Moreover, the direction is often obscure and the end is ever-changing.

Working with psychics is a delicate business and must be done with great consideration, understanding, and controls. Such activity is often very energy-consuming and debilitating. It can even be harmful.

To quote Fromm, the motivation must be "of the highest" and literally flow from "the love of humanity." To the anthropologist, morally relativistic by tradition, this will seem like an almost insurmountable proposition. Less than the highest motivation, however, seems but to lead the research down dark, devious, and unproductive alleyways in the maze of understanding. High motivation and faith, in my experience, are essential ingredients.

I began by stating that my study of intuitive archaeology started on the level of "fun and games." It has now become a quite serious matter. For the scientist in me, it is a humbling experience. . .and a shocking one. Pragmatically, the process seems to work a great deal of the time; thus, it is worthy of pursuit.

I recommend that it be pursued with a constant sense of scientific skepticism, while maintaining a sense humour, and that work be interspersed with periods of rest and relaxation for the purpose of keeping perspective and rebuilding and renewing the energies expended. Such work in the field of intuitive archaeology can, and I believe has, led and will lead to a richer and, hopefully, a more accurate understanding of human prehistory.

[This symposium was well-received, although I was told there was one dissenting paper in the symposium that argued for orthodoxy and putting aside this kind of speculation. The entire sym-

posium, including Dr. Emerson's talk, was later published in book form by Scarecrow Press under the editorship of Joseph K. Long.

Here also, written about this time, is an excerpt from Dr. Emerson's papers which further gives a feeling for what kind of man he was and how he experienced our ongoing research and the events that came into his life as a result.]

I am not the same person who began these studies two and a half years ago. Each passing day seems to have its impact and to initiate change. I very much sense that I am part of a situation and/or events which are part of a process or state of becoming—yet becoming just what I do not clearly see. The state of change is almost too fast and complex to grasp in a tangible, organized way.

Many things have happened which have almost daily urged me on in my pursuit. Much as I have endeavoured to follow a policy of go slow and take it easy, the whole matter seems to snowball and develop at an ever-increasing rate. There is something mysterious working behind the scenes that I find I cannot grasp and define, nor yet can I dismiss.

Events have proceeded forward in such a manner that I have developed a daily attitude of anticipation and expectancy—what will happen today that will help develop the program? A phone call? A letter? A new person that I will meet? An old friend with a relevant story to tell me? A challenging article? A new book that presents knowledge that is helpful? Something like this does happen almost daily.

Such events, as I have suggested, appear to be more than just coincidental and also seem to form a pattern. This raises the question, as I did in my initial representation: What is the ultimate purpose, the real priority, the possible and foreseeable end of this work? I am really no closer to an answer, for I seem —even myself—to be involved in a process of "becoming." But becoming *what* I do not know. Hopefully my work with George will contribute to a new kind of understanding of the prehistory of human beings.

Something that has constantly and recurrently impressed me as this work has progressed over two and a half years now is how many like-minded individuals I have met who are sympathetic and who have, in a quiet way, been contemplating, studying, and researching problems which, although seemingly unique and diverse, appear to have been along a parallel course.

These people come from all walks of life and represent and combine a great wealth and diversity of learning, expertise, and wisdom. They are thoughtful and thought-provoking people, and they are all fascinatingly human. Their work seems to be converging on a single theme: a new and vital understanding of man and his purpose and destiny in the Universe.

The song tells us this is the Age of Aquarius. Perhaps it is the predicted age of the development of the human spirit. I would like to be part of that kind of development in the years, days, and hours left to me; and perhaps I am already making a contribution, who knows? I certainly want to.

Chapter 11

Comments by George

I did not attend the meeting in Mexico City because my family and I had decided to move to Nanaimo, British Columbia, and so a trip that far away was out of the question. Dr. Emerson, from reports to me, made quite an impression with his paper, and he met many other people involved in parapsychology and some important and fruitful associations came out of it.

I, in the meantime, found myself busy with projects with other people interested in my work. It was surprising how many other archaeologists now contacted me to work on artifacts, although most asked to be unnamed and not to let others know they had been in touch with me. This included some from museums and universities throughout Canada and the United States and some overseas countries. I, of course, respected their wishes. This did not surprise me, as I had met many people who wanted my help but wished to remain unknown. It only proved the courage Dr. Emerson displayed when he publicly read a paper telling about his work with me and others.

Chapter 12

Intuitive Archaeology
and Related Matters
A Paper by Dr. Emerson

*[In March of 1975, Dr. Emerson arranged and chaired a symposium of papers on "Intuitive Archaeology and Related Matters."
This again was presented at the annual meeting of the Canadian
Archaeological Association, this time held in Thunder Bay, Ontario.
Dr. Emerson gave a paper in two parts. One was his Introductory
Statement. The other followed as a Summary after the other papers
had been presented.]*

Introductory Remarks

This 8th Annual Meeting of the Canadian Archaeological Association will mark a first in Canadian archaeology—the first time
that a complete session has been devoted to the subject of intuitive
archaeology. I sincerely hope that it will not be the last, but that
it will serve as a beginning and as an inspiration for future research.

In working with such research, the term "intuitive archaeology"
may well be restrictive. It will be evident from the papers presented
that the framework of study and analysis has already extended well
beyond the scope of both intuition and archaeology. That is because
the pursuit of such study tends to become characterized by a holistic
type of thinking that is both intra-disciplinary and inter-disciplinary
in the broadest sense of the words. Moreover it may well, in its
final formulation, be seen to embrace matters that are both traditionally "scientific" and traditionally "religious" and "spiritual" and
bring a new amalgam which could well be seen as "parascientific."

It will become evident from the presented papers that the research
reported is dealing with matters that can be stated in terms of energy
forces that are amenable to traditional conceptualization of electro-

magnetism, force fields, vibrations, sound and colour. Other manifestations will appear reasonable only in terms of newly-discovered or poorly-defined energy sources and their behaviour. It is also inevitable that the research will encounter events and happenings that appear understandable only in spiritual terms—events which have traditionally been explained as magic, witchcraft, superstition, "accidents," coincidence, and perhaps even "miracles."

The task of trying to cope with such matters scientifically will be the work of generations of research and will, I feel sure, seriously alter our views of the nature of science, culminating, perhaps, in either a new or a very old emergent view of man and his past, present, and even future place in the world and the galaxies which infinitely surround him.

My initial experience in this field, as most of you probably know, was with my friend and psychic informant George;[1] some of those activities will be reported to you today. In seeking to understand the information and guidance which he gave me relative to archaeological artifacts and sites, I chose to call the activity "intuitive," because what he told me was obviously not the product of a reasoned, educated, rational learning process, nor was it otherwise understandable in terms of his life experience. Rather, what he told me seemed to be "immediately known" and to a high degree accurate and true—at least 80 percent true. Such behaviour is comprehended by the term *intuitive*.

Encounters with the writings of Robert Orenstein[2] dealing with the neuro-physiology and the psychology of consciousness has drawn attention to the potential of human left-brain and right-brain functions. He conceptualizes the right brain as eternal, timeless, a-causal, simultaneous, and intuitive; the left hemisphere as time-oriented, causal, sequential, logical, intellectual, and rational in its functioning. Orenstein's thinking appeared to provide a basis for viewing George's performance in rather new ways.

At the same time, George's statements seemed to indicate that he was doing things other than just performing intuitively; he was recalling or relating events far back in time (retrocognition), he was seeing events taking place (clairvoyance), he was going up in the air to make observations while his physical body stayed on the ground (astral traveling), and he spoke of receiving symbolic and verbal messages (clairaudience and clairsentience). Such realization, combined with George's accuracy, was, as I have said, "mind-boggling."

In search of understanding and enlightenment, I found myself drawn to the field of parapsychology and the study of extrasensory perception and psi phenomena. Here a whole new intellectual world opened up, and it was being statistically demonstrated in controlled laboratory situations that there were humans who could predict dice throws and identify card selections well above chance expectations.

Reading Carl Jung, Arthur Koestler, and others[3] led me to consider the theories of "synchronicity" and the concept of "meaningful coincidences" as well as the unlikelihood of "chance" events and the likelihood of "miracles." Such a search—an intellectual search—led me to additional events which can only be described as "mysterious and unexplained." It was about that time that the writings of Carlos Castaneda were published to further complicate the situation.[4]

Dr. J.B. Rhine, who was interested in what I was trying to do—namely, to wed archaeology and parapsychology into a meaningful study of human prehistory—suggested from his background of wisdom that I perhaps might find it profitable to approach such work from the point of view of dowsing and divination. Here, at least, there was a substantial background of experience and documented research to draw upon.[5] This I did; two of the papers that will be presented today reflect this developing interest. Such research does have the advantage that it is testable and retestable and can be assessed pragmatically and perhaps explained in traditional scientific terms.

But as time went on I realized that matters were not that simple. The matter being investigated was really the problem of information generation by one means or another. I was studying a continuum which appeared to present a hierarchy of increased complexity from such phenomena as the Ouija board, teacup reading, crystal ball gazing and automatic writing to dowsing and divination; through psychometry, meditation, hypnosis, telepathy, astral travel and ultimately to trance mediumship and new levels of consciousness and perception.[6] It was and is an attractive, stimulating, and mysterious challenge that I hope some of you may come to share.

Such research is in the process of being taken seriously. I have recently returned from the 73rd Annual Meeting of the American Anthropological Association in Mexico City, where a whole session was devoted to the topic of "Parapsychology and Anthropology" which included, I am happy to say, three archaeological papers among the ten presented. The successful reception of this session has led to the planning of a second. The recognition of the need for including such studies in the scope of anthropology came from no less a scholar than Dr. Margaret Mead.

In my summary remarks I will have more to say about the potential of such research. To commence this session I will but quote from a famous scientist, Albert Einstein: "The most beautiful experience we can have is the mysterious. It is the fundamental emotion which stands at the cradle of true art and true science."[7]

* * * * *

Summary and Potential

I sincerely thank and commend those who have presented papers. They have had the courage to take a stand in a field that is, to say the east, debatable and controversial; to offer the convictions they feel; and to present the data they have encountered for serious consideration.

You have been exposed to pragmatic cases where the intuitive or psychic approach works—not perfectly, but it does work—and the *why* is a matter for speculation. You have also been exposed to well-documented cases of energy forces at work. You have been made aware of the impact of these forces upon human behaviour and have seen evidence that humans have sought to utilize and integrate such forces into their activities. Two facts stand out: the element of pragmatism and the wide scope of the matters to be studied. It is a rich, exciting, and developing field.

This work has, in a sense, been pioneered within the field of archaeology. In the time left, I would like to offer three examples to colleagues in the areas of ethnohistory, physical anthropology, and social anthropology for consideration because I am convinced that the use of the intuitive or psychic approach can be of value to them. The first example is related to ethnohistory.

On July 18, 1973, George and I visited the Warminister Site near Orilla, Ontario. Although George had no inkling of the site's importance, I had hoped that he would provide information that would help establish the fact that this was the capital village of the Hurons which was visited by Champlain in 1615. A small part of the 69-page text is here recapitulated:

> *Norman:* "Can you get any details on the white man leader you mentioned?"
> *George:* "Oh, the only detail I can get, they were French."

Norman: "That's a real good start."

George: "And they. . .well. . .he. . .when they arrived here. . .he. . .they all looked the same, damn near."

Norman: "The Frenchmen, they all looked pretty crummy, eh?"

George: "Yeah."

Norman: "Did they have any different types of hats?"

George: "No, they had bandannas, it appears."

Norman: "Bandannas?"

George: "They're stained you know, they had long pigtails down, too; and they were pretty scruffy when they arrived; during their stay here, which looks to be ten to 12 days."

Norman: "They stayed ten or 12 days?"

George: "And during their stay here the three of them appeared in real shiny clothes."

Norman: "Pretty fancy outfits?"

George: "With lace frills."

Norman: "No kidding?"

George: "Hanky. . ."

Norman: "Handkerchiefs and lace cuffs. Did they have high boots?"

George: "Yeah, high boots."

Norman: "No kidding?"

George: "They looked like silk stuff on 'em. Very. . .almost what you would call tapestry today."

Norman: "Yeah, right."

George: "And hat plumes."

Norman: "No kidding."

George: "There was a feather in it that the Indians had never seen before; they were quite taken with this, and it was quite an honour for the chief."

Norman: "Can you identify the feather?"

George: "It looks like ostrich."

Norman: "Ostrich? Probably is. . .I don't know I guess. . ."

George: "They were purple—dyed, you know."

Norman: "Purple?"

George: "The leader had. . .appears to be a coat, as I say, it dropped down and is flat across the bottom, almost like a topcoat today."

Norman: "Oh, a tail coat?"

George: "Breeches, vest, brocade, and it was maroon colour, vest and the rings, sword off the side in a scabbard, high boots, looked very 'pretty' to us."

Norman: "Sure."

George: "Goatee, you know."

Norman: "He had a goatee. Was he grey-haired?"

George: "He. . .he shows some grey."

Norman: "A bit of grey. . .eh?"

George: "The thing about him was when he arrived here he looked so. . ."

Norman: "So scruffy. . .eh?"

George: "But still he was a leader, he was a man used to control, being 'top dog.' He was. . .his actions. . .he was. . .educated, spirited."

Norman: "Can you get a picture of the time of year he arrived here?"

George: "It was coming on very late summer."

It is my conviction that George was describing Champlain, who did arrive in late summer. . .September 17, 1615. . .at Cahiague. Champlain did have two lieutenants. . .Etienne Brule and Thomas Godfrey. Champlain's records suggest that he stayed 15 days. George said that their stay "looked to be" ten or 12 days. A discrepancy. . .a matter of debate. But if Champlain was no more accurate at recording time than he was at estimating distance, there is room for argument.

The description of the leader could be that of many cavalier 17th-century Frenchmen, but Champlain and his party are the only white, non-religious men to visit the Hurons during that particular time in history. If George was not intuitively describing Champlain, I can only ask, who else?

I now address myself to my colleagues in physical anthropology. At the annual C.A.A. meeting in Whitehorse last year George consented, as a special concession to Pat Severs, to analyze a mandible and skull. Normally, George will have nothing to do with burial sites and human skeletal material if he can help it. The reading was witnessed by a group of archaeologists and physical anthropologists in our hotel room. The analysis covered an hour. There were many long pauses. I recapitulate but a part.

George: "The teeth are all wrong, aren't they."

Norman: "The teeth are all wrong?"

George: "The teeth are all wrong. That is what's hitting me."

Norman: "You mean they are not growing in the right way? Or the right order?"

George: "Well. . .yeah, he's only got a couple of maulers."

Norman: "He's got a funny jaw full of teeth, eh?"

George: "Yeah, I was just saying, there is only two maulers each side, that doesn't seem right. . .this fang tooth is not. . .he doesn't have a fang tooth. . .five points on the teeth. . .on the maulers. There's something trying to tell me something, and I can't get it."

Norman: "You're getting onto something there."

George: "I'm not getting . . . They had . . . one . . . two . . . three . . . four . . . five points on the tooth and that's supposed to be a grain . . . eating animal there, eh? But the funny part, I don't see the fang. That's supposed to be it right there . . . I don't know . . . only two maulers. There is no sign there would ever be a wisdom come in there . . .a lot different than they've seen, you know? . . . [long pause]. . .I am getting two trains of thought on this. I keep thinking it's a man, you know. But I'm being told it's not a man. Now they say first of all . . . it's a sub-human form of man, that's what I'm getting . . . but it can't be . . . This was not a meat-eating type . . . [very long pause] . . . Now I have to think about it for awhile. I'll come up with an answer in an hour."

Norman: "Okay."

George: "The fact that it doesn't have enough maulers. . .There isn't a man who doesn't have at least three of them; and it doesn't have pronounced eye teeth, you know. . .fang teeth here on this side. . .it doesn't have them. It suggests immediately that this here is a grain-eating animal because of the maulers, and the fact that the jaw swung down and the tongue also. . .it had its own channel here. . .only way it could. . .the depth of the jaw itself. They can't fathom it. . .big study. I've looked at it enough for them to know. I'm going to have to know. They're going to find out. I don't know."

Jim: "Would part of the problem at the moment be if it happens to be quite old?"

George: "Oh yeah, the age is one of those things, and the fact that usually in this case is because they are going further back, it isn't that I am unfamiliar with it..it's they are unfamiliar with it, you understand? I keep saying 'they,' but that is not the right term either."

Norman: "Would you say 'my informants'?"

George: "My source of information has to be enlightened, too. If it was something to do with Indians, they would pick it up faster, but it isn't Indian so I can't pick it up that fast, it is too far back. If it was something that was common knowledge, that wouldn't be too bad to dig out, but they are no bone experts."

This text demonstrates two things: George's intuitive competence at physical anthropology and some startling information upon his information sources. I emphasize that George has no familiarity with skulls and mandibles. However, he was able to observe and comment upon molar development and cusp patterns, the incisors, canines, and the mandibular taurus. His diagnosis of subhuman, Mongoloid, and grain-eating is interesting.

His performance impressed Pat Severs, a "confirmatory." Jim Burns and others present indicated they were impressed. In fact, I believe they were subject to the "deep personal shock" which I have suggested becomes almost routine in such psychic research when he casually spoke of his information sources who, he said, "are no bone experts."

It appears that George has contact with, or is sensitive to, a "research team" who search out information for him, correlate the data he gives them, and give him answers. In turn, they seem to have access to other specialists from whom they seek "enlightenment." In truth, we seem to be dealing with some dimension of other realities, which I hope may be of interest to those in physical anthropology.

I now turn to the field of social anthropology and recapitulate an excerpt from the statement George made about the black argillite carving from British Columbia upon which I last year reported in part.

Norman: "You were telling me that these people would collect a lot of stuff."

George: "When they got too many possessions, they invited a lot of people over and gave it away."

Norman: "Invited them all and gave it away? You indicated before why they gave it away. . .in other words, why did they get this stuff and why did they give it away?"

George: "Well. . ."

Norman: "They are not like us in that way, are they?"

George: "No, material things didn't. . .it was really to possess anything, to own anything was bad in that. . .well. . .it's really hard to describe. . .it's hard to understand. . .a man didn't have prestige when he didn't have anything. . .he. . .if you took stuff to him, it. . .oh, how can I describe this?"

Norman: "It isn't easy, because it is quite a bit different, isn't it?"

George: "It is quite a bit different, especially from the way I was brought up, that you have to possess things to become known as. . ."

Norman: "An important character?"

George: "Yes."

Norman: "A successful person?"

George: "A successful person, yeah. It was directly opposite. . .the most successful person was the one who had nothing because he could come and go as he pleased and not have to worry."

Norman: "He didn't have to worry?"

George: "He didn't have to worry, and the more he had, the more he had to answer for and every possession had a spirit, and you know every thing had a spirit. . .every chair, every leaf. . .you get what I mean, you didn't want to. . .well, it was difficult enough to live every day with nothing because even then you had to continually watch what you were doing so you weren't hurting the spirit. . .the wind spirit, the rain spirits, the sun spirit, the tree spirit. . ."

Norman: "Were you worried about hurting other people at all?"

George: "Yes, that's definite. Oh yeah, because that was a very important thing. . .I mean not only everything, but everybody had a spirit."

Norman: "Everybody had a spirit?"

George: "You had to watch that. . .an enemy or even a friend died. . .you certainly didn't want his spirit passing over there and passing the word around that you were a bum. That was no good."

Norman: "Is that right?"

George: "Yeah, you had to watch that."

Norman: "How could you protect against that?"

George: "You bet, you had to be nice to everybody; or just one Joe over there put in a bad word and you were black-balled, you know."

Norman: "This 'being nice' would involve giving him things, would it?"

George: "Yeah, to a sense. When you give somebody something, you gave him a whole pile of trouble because some day they were going to have to give it."

Norman: "They sort of took over on 'the trouble' for awhile?"

George: "That's right, that's right! They accepted it; and to have more than what you needed. . .that was a terrible thing. You just didn't do that. If you were a chief and had great possessions, that was terrible. You weren't a very good chief if you had all kinds of stuff. You were a great chief if you didn't have a lot of possessions. And it was a great thing for the head of one tribe to ask another tribe over and just give everything the tribe asked. It was a great thing that was good and. . ."

Norman: "A big do, eh?"

George: "Yeah, for the people who were coming, they were afraid not to come because they would antagonize this great chief, you know. When they got them there, they were not too damn happy when they gave them all that stuff, you know, cause next week they had to get some other guy at the other end, invite him and get rid of it. Just, they kept things moving, you know."

I want to emphasize that the above responses were triggered or generated by the black argillite carving which George was holding in his hand. Those of you who are familiar with the gift-giving ceremonial of the Northwest coast, "potlatch," will perhaps feel as I do that this was what George was describing in behaviourial terms. You will also recognize that the interpretation intensively given is rather different from that given by traditional anthropologists such as Ruth Benedict in *Patterns In Culture.*

It may be that social anthropologists have over-emphasized the prestige-gaining aspects of the ceremony and have under-emphasized the transfer of spiritual obligations so clearly delineated by George. Whatever the case, it suggests that such intuitive readings may well lead to reassessment of data and be of profit to social anthropology.

My final remarks are addressed to all who see themselves as seekers. . .seekers after truth. It is my conviction that we are on the verge of a new human revolution. . .one which may have proceeded further than any of us yet fully realize. We have had glimpses of it throughout human history; it has been manifested in the lives and utterances of great men, prophets, seers, sages, scientists, musicians, poets, artists, and world leaders.

In historical perspective, it can be argued that human development began under the guidance of intuition and revelation. This crystalized into the domination of the great world religions and their dogma. Much of this receded as the Dark Ages were replaced by the Age of Enlightenment, culminating in the dominance of science, technology, and the hardware that ultimately put man on the moon. But like the Dark Ages, this development has led to the erosion of human life and human values so manifest in the Western world today.

The revolution that I posit is the mergence of those things that have proven to be good in these two great historical traditions. . .the wedding or welding of intuition and science. Such a revolution is being spurred by the recognition of such men as George, who demonstrates that his "powers" are neither unique nor supernormal. . .that they are not a "gift," divine or otherwise, but that they are part and parcel of the human animal and go back to the dawn of prehistory.

Such a new human evolution is not only possible, but seems to be with us already in the cooperation of the scientist and the psychic and the great wave of interest that the general public is showing in everything of this nature. Perhaps ultimately there will be a emergence of both these strains in the ordinary human being. The impact of such mergence is prodigiously unpredictable. Our hope will be that it is for human good.

I believe that as we pursue such studies, we will encounter new forces which will draw us outward into the galaxies of infinite time and space to a new understanding of man in the mysterious, beautiful, and as yet unexplained scheme of things. I commend such studies to you with enthusiasm, caution, and humility.

References:

[1] J.N. Emerson, "Intuitive Archaeology, Psychic Approach," *New Horizons*, Vol. 1, No. 3 (January 1974). New Horizons Research Foundation, Box 427, Station F, Toronto 5, Ontario, Canada.

[2] Robert E. Orenstein, *The Psychology of Consciousness* (San Francisco: W.H. Freeman & Co, 1972).

[3]C.G. Jung, "The Structure and Dynamics of the Psyche," *Collected Works, Vol. VIII* (London: Tr. Hall, R.F.C.).

[4]Carlos Castaneda, *The Teachings of Don Juan* (New York: Ballentine Books, Inc., 1969); *A Separate Reality* (New York: Simon and Schuster, 1971); *Journey to Ixtlan* (New York: Simon and Schuster, 1972); *Tales of Power* (New York: Simon and Schuster, 1974).

[5]Guy Underwood, *The Pattern of the Past* (Toronto, Ontario: Pitman House, 1970).

[6]J.N. Emerson, "Intuitive Archaeology: A Developing Approach," presented at the Symposium "Parapsychology and Anthropology," November 23, 1974, at the 73rd Annual Meetings of the American Anthropological Association in Mexico City. Symposium to be published, edited by Joseph K. Long.

[7]Albert Einstein, *Ideas and Opinions* (New York: Crown Publishers, Inc., 1954).

Chapter 13

Comments by George

Upon reading these remarks given by Dr. Emerson, you will notice how far we had come in our work together. We had now become a team and it was serious business rather than a weekend hobby. Dr. Emerson had now immersed himself and me in projects on a weekly basis when time permitted.

Norman had picked me up at my home in Peterborough, Ontario, with his camper van and we went to the area around Orillia, Ontario, about a hundred miles away. We arrived in the middle of a pasture off the highway, north of Orillia. Dr. Emerson said we would camp here for the night and in the morning walk to an Indian site not too far from where we were. We were parked on a rough trail of some kind that led to a ravine with brush in it. Near the camper was an old stone foundation that Dr. Emerson asked me about.

I told him it was an old barn from the time of the original pioneer people and the stones had come from a stream bottom and bank nearby. He then asked me if I felt anything about the area. I told him I felt a great sadness to do with native people. He asked me to explain exactly what it was. I told him that somewhere nearby a lot of Indian people had lost their lives because of the white man. He showed a little surprise and asked me to go on, but I could not, because I felt so sad and it was getting late at night. I told him I would probably feel more like talking when we were on the site in the morning.

We awoke early in the morning and enjoyed a good breakfast of eggs, bacon, coffee, toast, and jam, all prepared by Dr. Emerson, who took delight in doing it.

We left the camper where we had parked it the night before and walked along the path. When we had reached the ravine, I found a small stream running through it. It was not difficult to cross over and we entered a clearing on the other side. I found myself face to face with an Indian who was standing there. He said, "It took you long enough to get here." I told Norm this and, though he looked surprised, he said nothing.

I had never had contact with this Indian before, and I was to find out later his name was Red Snake. He showed some reluctance to talk or communicate, but he did open up as we went along. He did not trust Norm or any other white person and came to me only because of my past encounters with others.

I now had the difficulty of listening to him in one world and Norman in another, which always confuses me, to say the least. If I was confused, how do you think Red Snake and Emerson felt? Norm asked questions and Red Snake answered something completely different. It was an hour before I had things sorted out enough to answer Norm and still keep my guide's attention.

He told me that this had been a great city of the Hurons; that up to 8,000 thousand people lived here at one time, depending on the time of year.

He showed me where the longhouses had been and where they had their palisades. He told me how they had expanded the longhouses and how they were forced to rebuild the palisades as the village expanded and where they had gardens and how they had to clear land to make more gardens. He also showed me where the Old Ones (the original inhabitants) had been buried and told me that now this was considered a sacred place. . .also, the new burial site at the top of the hill back of the village.

During all this, Emerson walked along with me asking questions in his quiet way and seeming to know there was another presence, but never indicating this. Norm always asked the right questions at the right time and would not push if he could see that I was not really with him. After about three hours of walking over, up, and down hills, Dr. Emerson and I were a little weary. We sat down on an old bench left there by the archaeological team that had worked there in the summer.

As we sat there this warm summer morning, Norm questioned me at length about the village and its inhabitants. He then asked me if there had been any white men there, and I replied that there had been Frenchmen here and I showed him where they had landed with their canoes and Indian guides. I also showed him where the lodge they had stayed in while they were there had stood.

I explained the negotiations that went on, in getting the village to join them in their war with the other Iroquois to the south of the Great Lakes. I did tell him of the return of the white people after their war and about the exploring done during the winter and the following spring and early summer by the French and their hosts. I went into detail about what happened after the white men left.

I must mention that the population in Cahiague varied with the seasons. During the winter there were about 8,000 people but in the summer there were only about 5,000. This does not take into account the 500 dogs and some two billion fleas that infested them and the fur clothing and bedding.

It was now early afternoon and Dr. Emerson and I left the village and returned to the camper where we had lunch. We left this area at about six that afternoon. This was not the last I saw of Red Snake, as we became friends and still are. We discussed the village for many weeks after, and Norm got more information as time went on. He seemed pleased that I had performed well. The knowledge of the site, which he had gathered when he had excavated it for several years before, could be used to judge my accuracy.

In the latter part of his paper, Dr. Emerson discussed the skull and lower jawbone that was given to me to look at in Whitehorse at the annual meeting of the C.A.A. The temperature was about 42 degrees below zero outside the hotel room, but it was a bright and sunny day. There seemed to be about 20 people in the room and I did not know who they were. All I was aware of was that they were colleagues of Dr. Emerson's and he wanted me to show them what I could do.

Even though I felt repulsed by handling another person's skull, I went ahead with it due to the circumstances. I knew the skull was quite old when I picked it up. This was the second time in my life that I had handled a skull.

It is not the most pleasant pastime, believe me. The first time was when Dr. Emerson brought a skull to Peterborough and asked me to look at it. It was an old one from the Battle of Hastings in England, from about 1066. The person who owned that skull was not a very good fighter because there was a hole in the skull from an operation to relieve the pressure from being hit on the head. The wound was pretty well healed over when he was hit again near the same place and this had healed over too. But another blow to the head had killed him. I told Dr. Emerson he was lucky it did before something bad happened to him, with his luck. I don't think he really appreciated my injecting humour into the work just then.

The skull in Whitehorse, as I have said, was very old and complex to work on. I placed its age as being somewhere around 6,000 years. I also thought at first that it was a female, then realized it was a small male person.

I had a feeling it was more Oriental than Indian and said so. I continually got up to wash my hands because I had a feeling of something contaminated, but this could have been because the person had died of a disease. My informants could not get all the information that was needed. I think perhaps this was because this skull was from long before their time. They did, however, do some analysis on it and, with the help of others, came through with some information.

The people in the room seemed satisfied with this, and even surprised in some way. After we left Whitehorse, Dr. Emerson and I went to Edmonton where he gave a lecture and then on to Saskatoon to the university there. While there I saw the rest of the artifacts that had been found near the skull. What I had said about it apparently corresponded with what was believed at the time.

(Left) Norm and Ann Emerson
George and Charlotte McMullen

Archaeologists working a dig at Mareau, Egypt,
where excavation has exposed walls.

(Left to right) Stephan Schwartz, Dr. Harold Edgerton,
George McMullen examining one of Professor Edgerton's graphs.
Alexandria, Egypt, Spring 1979.

(Left to right) Stephan Schwartz, George McMullen, Glen Winters (cameraman), in a Jewish graveyard in Alexandria, Egypt. George is drawing a picture of how it looked in Alexander's time.

(Left to right) Glen Winters, Stephan Schwartz, George McMullen in an ancient Mosque (c. A.D. 500) under present-day Nebs Daniel Mosque, Alexandria, Egypt.

Raymond Worring and George McMullen on Black Mesa, Montana.

Stephen Schwartz and George McMullen consulting during an excavation in Egypt. It appears that McMullen has given Schwartz something to think about.

Chapter 14

Archaeology, Parapsychology, and One White Crow
Excerpts from a Paper by Dr. Emerson

[The next of Dr. Emerson's papers was given at the invitation of the Florida Association for Psychical Research in Clearwater, Florida, in April 1975. Because it was for an entirely different audience, understandably much of it repeated what had been given in Ontario talks. For purposes of this book, then, I have deleted those sections of his talk, along with a section that will appear in a later paper. The part I am leaving in shows how his thinking had progressed.]

William James, the respected founder of American psychology, studied the American psychic Leonora E. Piper. He started out to debunk Mrs. Piper and ended up by declaring her to be his One White Crow. Dr. James stated, "If I may employ the language of the Professional Logic Shop, a universal proposition can be made untrue by a particular instance. If you wish to upset the law that all crows are black, you need not show that no crows are; it is enough to prove that one single crow is white."

Dr. James was convinced that the information given to him by Mrs. Piper was "never gained by the ordinary waking use of her eyes and ears and wits." Her performance defied the current rules of the psychology of learning. Dr. James confessed that he did not have "the glimmer of an explanatory suggestion to make" as to the source of her knowledge. Faced by this puzzling information, he confessed, "From admitting the *fact* of such knowledge I can see no escape."

In June 1971, I met my own One White Crow, my friend and psychic informant, George McMullen. He gave me information that, like Mrs. Piper's, did not seem to be gained by the ordinary waking use of his eyes, ears, or wits. Like Dr. James, I could see no escape from admitting the fact of such knowledge.

* * * * *

The accuracy of George's information was impressive. My One White Crow was providing me with information and knowledge that empirically and pragmatically spoke for itself, and, for me, there was no escape from the fact of such knowledge. These findings and many others led me to report to my Canadian archaeological colleagues the conviction that I had received knowledge and archaeological sites from a psychic informant who relates this information without any evidence of the conscious use of reason.

There were many who could not bring themselves to accept this data and argued that George must have gained this information from his learning, his reading, or his life experiences. His method of getting information ran contrary to currently accepted ideas about psychological learning theory. I can only state that George was uneducated and uninformed about matters of Ontario Iroquois archaeology. He had terminated his academic schooling at grade eight, although he had finished high school in a technical course. He was not a reader. He preferred to spend his leisure time in such pursuits as fishing and playing cards.

As my work progressed and I used other psychic informants to verify George's work, it appeared that I had encountered a whole flock of White Crows. In presenting my work to my colleagues, I stated, "This paper holds that intuitive or psychic knowledge stands as a viable alternative to the knowledge obtained by the more traditional methods of science."

In calmer retrospect, this was heady and heretical stuff! It was almost as if, in my enthusiasm, I was suggesting to my traditional scientific colleagues, "Why don't you take a rest and my psychics and I will provide you with the 'real' story of man's prehistory and, for that matter, solutions to other scientific problems—if you will but give us a chance"—although that was not what I intended to convey.

I had arrived at a point where I had considerable respect for the White Crows that I had discovered amongst the otherwise black-crow population and was sure that there would be more who would appear if they were assured an unbiased hearing. I felt that I had been able to present my colleagues with at least some facts from which they could not escape; they might not like them, but they could not deny them.

But skepticism will recede only very slowly, and that includes my own. And so it was with great satisfaction that at the 1975 meeting of the Canadian Archaeological Association I was able to chair a complete session with eight papers presented on the topic of "Intuitive Archaeology and Related Matters." I no longer felt like a lone voice crying out in a psychic or intuitive wilderness. The gradual buildup and accumulation of such evidence will serve to demonstrate the reality and credibility of people like George and others to a point where they will have to be taken seriously.

The most exciting information I have received on this topic was a research proposal prepared by an electrical engineer and mathematician with 25 years' experience with the Stanford Research Institute. It was entitled "A Creative Information Service for Scientific Speculation." The objective of the proposed endeavour was "To better utilize human creative potential for the solution of important scientific technical problems." The methodology proposed was: "Creative ideas will be gathered and catalogued from two sources: eminent scientists and people known as psychics who have, in the past, demonstrated their ability to make *meaningful* scientific contributions through use of their creative potential. Initial research will address itself to the important fields of: (1) Seismology, (2) Food Synthesis and Production, and (3) Theoretical Physics (including Energy Sources)."

Should this initial program prove successful, I was most pleased to note that it might be expanded to include archaeology, as well as linguistic mental processes, microbiology, brain function (at the level of cells and cell assemblies), birth control, and many other topics. This presents a spectacular opportunity for the cooperation of the psychic and the scientist—something I feel that George and I have been pursuing with some degree of success.

To me, such acceptance shows the beginnings of a willingness to look at the ever-growing evidence that human beings are capable of perceiving other levels of reality and utilizing altered states of consciousness and new levels of perception—all part of a new area of developing science as White Crows accumulate in increasing numbers and their presence and abilities become known.

Black crows are clever, sensitive, and highly intelligent birds, a fact to which the seasoned hunter will attest. Perhaps White Crows will prove an inspiration, and although this may confound traditional science, it will be of great interest to those dedicated to exploring the far reaches of man's mind as he explores his inner and outer being to find its true place in the cosmos and the eternities past, present, and future; in time and space, as the galaxies are searched out and probed by new and exciting methodologies and open minds look at the inescapable evidence that is coming through.

Chapter 15

Comments by George

It is apparent that Dr. Emerson and I had covered a lot of ground since we first met. Both of us learned a great deal from our research together. I don't know whether I like being a White Crow or not. It means I will stick out in a crowd of black crows, whereas I would like to blend in with the others. That I am a White Crow does not mean I am different or know more than the black ones. There is one thing for sure—a crow is a crow; it doesn't make any difference what colour you are.

By this time Dr. Emerson had become a person dedicated to the research of the parapsychological and how it would benefit the discipline he had been trained in. He never worried that he may be ridiculed or even scorned by his colleagues. His was a determination to get answers, and he had the courage of his convictions.

We had many trips and he taped them all. Unfortunately, most of the tapes have not been transcribed, due to his untimely death. Hopefully, in time they will be. I can remember three such research trips we made that have not yet been mentioned in his papers.

On a trip to Thunder Bay, Ontario, to attend a meeting of the Canadian Archaeological Association, we were invited by a local anthropologist to examine a site he had worked on. Dr. Emerson and I, with two or three other archaeologists, went to a site not far from Thunder Bay. There was about three inches of snow covering the ground and the weather was cold.

At the site Dr. Emerson asked for my comments. I told him this was a very old site used just as the ice was receding after the last Ice Age. I described the type of plants and shrubs growing and that the lake shore, now some 30 miles away, was then within feet of where we were standing. I told him this was not a permanent living area, but one used to gather and make flint tools and I told him there was a strata of flint about 18 inches wide on the hillside behind where we were standing. Later, the archaeologist who had worked the site confirmed that what I had said was true. That did not surprise Norman, but impressed the others who had come along.

The next project came when we were in Whitehorse attending another meeting of the C.A.A. We arrived there on a Friday night and had a chance to renew acquaintances with some people we had come to know at other meetings. It had been arranged that Dr. Emerson and I were to be on an open-line radio show the next morning. This was a local station and we were to be on for half an hour starting at 10:00A.M. We arrived on time and after the half hour was up the people asked us to stay another half-hour as the response was so heavy. We not only stayed the extra half-hour, we were kept there for the full two hours of the program because the interest was so great.

After lunch we had an interview with the local newspaper, which lasted about an hour. I then took a walk. It was about 40 below zero so walking was not great. I happened to pass the local museum and found it was closed. This I could not understand; with so many of Canada's most important anthropologists, archaeologists, physicists, and others in town, why would it be closed? I took the phone number from a sign on the door and when I returned to the hotel I phoned the museum people. They assured me that they would open the museum at 6:00 that evening until 10:00 so we could all see the native exhibits. I relayed the message to Dr. Emerson, who had it announced over the hotel intercom.

We then had a visit to our room by a man from the Museum of Man in Ottawa, Ontario. He had a few artifacts for me to psychometrize. Most were just mundane and I had no difficulty with them. But one was a puzzler; it was a fish hook made of bone, with one piece missing. The difficulty was that I saw it being used to make a net of dried gut and sinew. Neither Dr. Emerson nor our guest had ever seen such a net before and questioned my findings.

Later that evening at the local museum, I found such a net hanging there and Dr. Emerson and the man from the National Museum agreed that I had been right. Also while there I saw a stuffed timber wolf and I was surprised at the size of this monster. They assured me that this was the usual size of these animals. No wonder the Indian had such respect for wolves.

Later in the evening we had been asked to go to a local coffee house to meet some people. It turned out to be hangout for the local kids. We had a cup of something thick, black, and bitter, which I would not describe as coffee. While we were there, a young man approached me and offered me a pill which he said would expand my mind and make my ability ten times better. I refused with thanks and later I was told he was a writer who had been there for some three years expanding his mind. If he stayed there much longer he would have to get a bigger head.

When my wife Charlotte and I, along with Ann and Dr. Emerson, were traveling in the United States, we visited Ann's sister in Connecticut. We were invited to visit a friend of Lee's who was a researcher working on a book for a prominent author. She was researching one of Brigham Young's 27 wives, Ann Eliza Young, and could not find out what had happened to her after she vanished from the pages of history in 1908. She had been in no small way responsible for the U.S. government's crackdown on the Mormon's Utah community, abolishing polygamy and stripping the elders of all but one wife. She had made many enemies within the faith.

The researcher asked me to pyschometrize the book Ann Eliza had written, called *My Life In Mormon Bondage*, but I refused. However, when she left the room I touched the book. When she returned, I told her no good purpose would be served in her or anyone else's finding out what had happened to Ann Eliza. Later I told Dr. Emerson, because he was my trusted friend, that she had died in the desert in Utah or Arizona. She had been terribly persecuted by her friends and relatives and perhaps Young's other wives. She had been kept on the desert until she finally went out of her mind. It was not a pretty story.

After the researcher returned to the room, she began to explain Mormonism to me. Suddenly I took over the discussion, sounding (I was later told) like a Mormon patriarch, arguing on behalf of Young and the Mormon's ethic, defending it, describing in close detail what had happened in the community before and after the U.S. government intervened so brutally. I made it sound that Ann Eliza had to atone for all the pain she had brought on the community. I found myself defending their practice of having several wives, even though it is much against my everyday beliefs. Dr. Emerson said later that he knew I was an authority on Indians but didn't know I was an authority on Mormons. I told him I wasn't until I touched the book.

What I tried to emphasize was that her actions had disrupted the whole Mormon community, their beliefs, and their way of life. When the government in its haste seized the property of the Mormons, they took some of the money and built a shelter for the wives they had displaced. These women were taken here against their will and after a short time left the shelter and returned to their community, where they were happy to be in the first place.

It is hard to understand why the government did this on the complaint of one woman. There appeared to be a conflict between the freedom to practice the religion of one's choice and the morals of the people represented by the government. I am sure the government wished it had not heard of the whole matter and wanted it to quietly disappear.

I am no authority on any religion, nor am I a religious person. I am a moral person and I try to do what is right. I was brought up in the Christian faith but have attended many other denominational churches. I respect them all for the good they do mankind. I have a saying: "It doesn't matter what you are as long as you are a good one."

I was approached at a meeting in Edmonton, Alberta, by a young woman and her boyfriend. She asked me if the man Joseph Smith really did find those tablets of gold that the Mormon church is based on. She told me she had been raised in the Catholic religion but had joined the Mormon church.

I told her that if I did know I would not tell her because she had to find out for herself. She had become unhappy with the Catholic faith because she was not satisfied. Now she was questioning the Mormon faith because she was still not satisfied. I told her she must keep on searching until she knew within herself what the truth was and was happy with it. I also told her she should consider the fact that she was living within her own church and the Holy Spirit was there within her.

We now come to what was to me the most disturbing trip of all. . .to Egypt and Iran with the Edgar Cayce Foundation.

Chapter 16

How We Became Involved With
the Edgar Cayce Foundation

As Norman's and my work progressed, he was often interviewed by the press and his work was written up in papers and journals across the country. There were a number of invitations to give talks. After he gave an informal one at an Esoteric Conference in Toronto, one of the attenders, who was making a trip to take part in a conference at the headquarters of the Association for Research and Enlightenment in Virginia Beach, Virginia, told Hugh Lynn Cayce, President of the A.R.E., about the talk he had heard.

The Association carries on the work of the late Edgar Cayce, widely known as "The Sleeping Prophet." He had left more than 14,000 readings given in a trance state, the bulk of which referred to people's physical ailments and often quite-miraculous healings which had resulted from following the advice given.

Hugh Lynn had long spearheaded the work of preserving the records his father had left—seeing that they were transcribed, collated, and secured, and making them available to a wide audience. He had made possible and supervised the publication of numerous books on various aspects of his father's psychic genius. He had built up a centre and a staff to give seminars and workshops. He had now completed most of the work that he felt needed to be done in connection with the physical readings and wanted to turn his attention to the small fraction of the data that dealt with other subjects, particularly the past-life readings his father had given sparingly and on request.

These gave fascinating information on ancient sites, civilizations, and Biblical and historical events. Hugh Lynn was especially interested in a reading that said his father had a lifetime in ancient Persia—now Iran. Here, according to the readings, his father had been a tribesman named Ultjed. He had been out in the wastelands with a female companion and they had been overcome by the sun.

They had managed to find a cave and had crawled in, more dead than alive. It turned out that there was a healing spring in this cave and the two were able to regain their health and strength.

Ultjed had then founded a healing and teaching centre there, which was called The City of the Hills and Plains and eventually had died and was buried in a cave there. Hugh Lynn had been to the area—it was described as being a certain number of miles from the modern town of Shustar. He had found remains of settlements, but wanted to be sure which one might be the one he was seeking. He felt that a psychic, especially one teamed with an archaeologist, could perhaps help him make this find.

He telephoned Dr. Emerson and asked if he could meet with him the next time he and I were together. Norman was intrigued; Cayce had been the means of his meeting me and beginning his work, since Ann had met Charlotte at an Edgar Cayce Study Group. He readily agreed. However, by this time I had moved to British Columbia.

The opportunity for the meeting had come when Norman gave his paper in Whitehorse on the argillite carving. While in the west, he came to visit me in my new home near Nanaimo. Hugh Lynn and his wife Sally, along with Arch Ogden, President of the Edgar Cayce Foundation, and his wife Ann, came to visit me in my new home. You can perhaps appreciate how awed Charlotte was to be asked to entertain such eminent people, especially when Ann Emerson was not there to give her support.

After getting acquainted and chatting to put everyone at ease, Hugh Lynn put a pile of artifacts on our dining room table and asked me to see what I could do with them. I separated them into three piles. I then began to speak about the first grouping. I apparently described the terrain and what was there so accurately that Hugh Lynn knew that I was talking about Elijah's Well, where he had picked up the fragments he had given me.

For the second site, I said I saw Roman legions going by and so designated it as a Roman site, which was apparently correct.

I then proceeded to work with the third grouping, describing the people as having funny helmets that looked like "upside-down funnels" and long, curved swords that were triangular in cross-section. It was immediately evident that I was describing the Saracens, whose site it was.

Obviously I had performed satisfactorily. Ann Ogden drew Charlotte aside and told her, "This man is really good." Hugh Lynn and Arch consulted and then asked Norman and me if we would be willing to accompany them on an expedition they were planning to Egypt and Iran. They said we would be needed on the Iranian leg of the journey.

This was how the expedition came about. Dr. Emerson and I, after a long consultation, consented to go. We paid our wives' fares so that they could come along and give moral support. At first Hugh Lynn did not feel we would be needed in Egypt because at that time it was at war with Israel and so not much could be done there; but he eventually decided to include us in that part of the trip. It was an extremely interesting one.

Chapter 17

Intuitive Archaeology: Egypt and Iran
An Article by Dr. Emerson

[Following the trip to Egypt and Iran, Norman wrote an article that was published in the A.R.E. Journal *in 1976. It follows.]*

Operationally, intuitive archaeology is, in essence, a simple and straightforward matter. For some years now, my friend and psychic informant, George McMullen, had demonstrated that he could hold objects in his hand, tune in to them, and apparently move back in time and space in order to relate to me where and when the object was an important part of a particular culture or in the life of a certain individual. He then describes for me the person, the place, and the use and significance of the object, quite often supplying descriptions of missing parts or attachments, and customs and happenings in the lives of the people who created or used the item.

George can also do the same type of thing while walking over an archaeological site. It appears as if he can project himself back in time and space to witness events that took place long ago and can see a place as it was when it was occupied by a now-vanished people.

The important fact that gradually emerged was that, not only could George do this, but he was doing it accurately. This accuracy could be assessed and tested by checking his statements against our established ethnohistoric and archaeological knowledge, and also against the results of follow-up excavation. These conditions of testability, verification, and assessment have given the study of intuitive archaeology credibility which has not been so readily evident in other areas of intuitive and psychic studies. For this reason I often state that "the proof is in the digging." I have come to welcome the opportunity to pursue such studies.

On October 20, 1974, an opportunity arose to carry out investigations in this area. At that time I met Mr. Hugh Lynn Cayce,

President of the A.R.E.—the Association for Research and Enlightenment in Virginia Beach, Virginia. His father, the late Edgar Cayce, renowned as "The Sleeping Prophet," had, during his lifetime, given a wealth of psychic information on a wide variety of subjects, including a number of statements about Near Eastern prehistory and archaeology. Having learned of my work in intuitive archaeology, Hugh Lynn wanted to know whether or not I felt George could help in his search for certain sites his father had described in the Near East. He felt that if one of these could be found and excavated, it would prove to be an event of considerable importance. To me it was an intriguing problem and worthy of a try.

We agreed that the next useful step would be a psychometric session. This took place in George's home at Nanaimo, British Columbia, on June 16, 1975. I was able to arrange my summer teaching schedule so as to be present with George. . .largely for moral support. He was nervous and underwent a number of tension-filled, sleepless nights as his intuitive and psychic resources were marshalled to cope with these Old World problems, novel to him.

The day arrived and so did Hugh Lynn, Mr. Arch Ogden, Director of the Edgar Cayce Foundation, and their wives, Sally and Ann, respectively. Immediate and positive rapport was established.

Hugh Lynn had brought eight small artifacts, samples collected from sites in the Mediterranean area, each comprised of a few broken potsherds with an occasional item of metal or glass. These were laid out on George's dining room table. Notes were taken and tape recordings made of George's observations.

He gave excellent readings. He soon correctly put these sites together as coming from the area of Mt. Carmel. One he described with such accuracy that Hugh Lynn was able to assess it as a description of Elijah's Well. Site by site, George gave details of terrain, animal and plant life, buildings, dress, customs, and lifeways that were "evidential." He included such interesting and convincing information as that the Carmelite Order took vows of chastity which set them apart and a detailed description of what could only be a particular type of Persian sword.

Mr. Cayce and Mr. Ogden were pleased both with the calibre of George's intuitive work and with George himself. An invitation was given for George and me to follow up this psychometric session with an expedition to Iran and possibly to Egypt. I was happy to be given the opportunity to work with the A.R.E., whose motivations and integrity I considered to be outstanding. My own research had convinced me that in intuitive studies the problem of motivation was one of extreme importance—that it must be "of the highest," and be directed toward the good of humanity.

In our research we have received requests and proposals to become involved in a variety of schemes. It has become my practice to scrutinize the motivation which seems to be involved and to politely reject those which appear to involve greed or personal gain. As I was to learn in greater detail, the highest of motivation characterizes the A.R.E. and its members.

In considering the Egyptian-Iranian expedition, George and I felt we could not accept the immediate and usual motives—that it would be fun and exciting to visit new and strange places in fascinating old lands. Nor did we want to use it as an ego trip to a "hot" psychic area where so many psychic studies were investigating the pyramids and writing about them.

George did not easily make the decision to participate. He felt at once he wanted to go, but he was far from happy about it. He saw it as something "he had to do." He felt that he would be visiting places where the Greatest of All Time had walked. The prospect seemed to be frightening and threatening to him, so he said he was consumed by an intense feeling of loneliness that he could scarcely put into words. . .that this was where it was all at; here was where the Great Ones had been and that he had to go. In his own way he prepared himself for this at the cost of many sleepless nights.

My problems were much less severe. Like other researchers in the field of intensive studies, I had long since become convinced that man was already deep in the beginning stages of a spiritual revolution which was manifesting itself in changes in human nature, happening all around us in many forms. I had come to accept the viewpoint that in my small way I was helping to demonstrate and document this and that was a positive and relevant motivation for me.

The problems we were to pursue had come from the psychic readings of Edgar Cayce, whom I considered to be a very spiritual man, a prominent and leading figure in this spiritual revolution that I sensed taking place. I concluded that whatever George and I could do to add to his credibility would be for the good of humanity and a worthy thing to attempt.

I felt this credibility, which I had never questioned, could be augmented in at least two ways. First, it might be possible that artifact and on-the-site psychometry readings by George would generate statements which would tend to confirm and complement the Cayce readings and in this way verify the work of both. Second, by being physically on the spot, it seemed possible that George could pinpoint the location of a site or of sites described in the Cayce readings and that a planned excavation program could be formulated for follow-up investigation which would perhaps yield solid proof in terms of material objects.

In addition, it seemed to me that the journey to Egypt and Iran would provide an excellent opportunity to further my studies with and of George, and for that matter of myself, in the area of intuitive archaeology. We would be faced with a whole new and novel set of conditions and circumstances that would provide us with a shift of research area from the New World to the Old. I felt that my own interests and those of Hugh Lynn Cayce were capable of integrating.

Once agreement was reached, plans proceeded. George arranged to take the time off from his job. Through the good offices of my chairman and dean, I was able to make arrangements to be away for most of the month of October. On October 7, 1975, accompanied by our wives, we flew to New York and joined the expedition which was to number from ten to 14 members in the 20 days we were together.

At no point were the aims and objectives of the expedition clearly and specifically stated, at least as I saw them. The nature of the research was open-ended and unstructured, and pressures were reduced to a minimum except that we did have a fairly intense timetable to keep. We followed a prearranged itinerary of times, places, accommodations, and meetings with interested people.

It was clearly stated that participation at each point was voluntary. In most cases, members of the party or each group seemed to be doing their own things, and it was not always clear just what those were! However, there grew up a generally shared attitude that we were all seeking "enlightenment" and would pursue it in whatever way we could. This led, at times, to considerable discussion and exchange of information and experiences. Each person was concerned about and considerate of the other members of the party.

At first, at least. this unstructured approach was disturbing and frustrating to me. It devastated my sense of exerting any scientific control. I had arrived in Egypt with almost no organized plan of attack, and none was offered. At times I found myself depressed and feeling like an outsider and a non-participant in the ongoing activities.

Despite the sometimes leisurely schedule, I found it hard to find opportunity to collect and assess my thoughts. Sometimes I felt myself to be extraneous and a stranger apart. Worst of all, there were times when I found myself annoyed, angry, and irritated with my friend George, whose lack of communication for periods of time I found to be almost insufferable. For days he would say nothing, or at least little that appeared relevant.

I was to learn that George, too, was being subjected to his own frustrations. Especially in Egypt he said he was being shown or told only so much by his psychic informants. He said that it was almost as if he were in a corridor with high walls on each side and that he was frustrated by not being able to see over them and not knowing when he would be permitted to see.

He was told this was not his territory and his intuitive and perceptive powers were being controlled. He was warned against visiting the King's Chamber in the Pyramid of Cheops. When he did go there, he said it felt as if the top of his head was being drawn upwards, and he could stay only a very short time. And so there was a problem of organization, of objectives, and of. . .for want of a better term. . . "psychic vibrations" with which to be coped. In the long run, the surprising thing is that the whole matter went so well.

I have commented in earlier papers that I was developing an awareness that my research was "being led" and that I am often presented with data in a manner which I have described as "meaningful coincidences." These, in turn, seem to merge into a pattern of understanding that appears to be beyond the normal chance probabilities of their having just occurred. This was certainly true of the Egyptian and Iranian work.

This recognition, as it grew, had a calming influence on me, as I realized that my role was more at that point a patient collector of data, rather than any active, vital director of research. Thus, I accepted the role of walking doggedly along behind George in the stifling heat, lugging my heavy tape recorder in the consistent hope that useful statements would be generated for future study. They were.

The Egyptian Phase of the Study

Six and one-half days were set aside for the Egyptian part of the trip. Apart from seeking information about a rectangular structure appended to the back left-hand side of the Sphinx, I had arrived in Egypt with no specific problem in mind. Hugh Lynn seemed to see George's presence in Egypt largely as a warm-up period for the Near East and time to whet his intuitive abilities for the more important tasks he faced in Iran. He was, in fact, anxious that George should not "burn himself out" working on Egyptian matters.

Thus, our involvement in the Egyptian phase of the work was almost an afterthought, although we were made very welcome. From the first, I considered George's presence in Egypt important and at the first meeting had stated my conviction that while I did not know what George would have to say, whatever it was would be important. Such proved to be the case.

Following a method which negated my sense of scientific control, George followed what I can only call a process of "intensive immersion" in matters of Egyptian archaeology and prehistory. In this, I accepted the point of view held by some that a psychic or intuitive person should have everything possible going for him in his search for answers, and so no sources of information should be barred. This immersion program began with a visit to the Cairo Museum, where George was exposed to the fabulous display of funeral goods from the tomb of Tutankhamen and to the shockingly and grotesquely displayed specimens in the Hall of Mummies.

The same day was devoted to a tour of the Sphinx area of Giza, where we taped a commentary of what George had to say on the Sphinx and its environment. The next stop was Luxor, including a 150-kilometre side trip to Abydos, the site of a temple and healing spring complex and the possible site of origin for the Cult of Osiris.

We returned to Luxor that evening in time to attend the spectacular sound and light display centred upon the colossal columns, statues, and structures that make up the temples of Karnak. The next day we took a boat trip across the Nile to visit the Valley of the Kings. This involved a descent into the tombs of Seti 1, Tutenkamun, and a third, less important Egyptian official.

We returned to Cairo and the Mena House, and the next day George and I took a camel ride to the Pyramids of Kufu and of Cheops. These both involved tiring ascents and descents into the interiors of these structures. We rejoined the others at the Pyramid of Cheops. The group again climbed to the King's Chamber at the apex of the structure, where a number of members stayed for a meditation session with varied and interesting results. George and I avoided this session because of the forces adverse to him.

That was George's five-day process of immersion into Egyptian archaeology, and on the sixth day he tape-recorded a summary statement for Hugh Lynn Cayce and me. It was generalized and to a large extent dwelt upon matters of a religious and philosophical nature. As one might suspect, he also raised a number of highly mysterious matters, such as water systems to the pyramids that flowed uphill not downward; and in typical George fashion, he took the stance, "I cannot understand it, but I am not going to argue with what I see."

He also described the location of a system of water channels, pools, fountains, and bathrooms replete with luxurious vegetation in the area immediately adjacent to the Sphinx that have been largely overlooked or at least not much discussed in traditional Egyptology. Hugh Lynn indicated that a number of the ideas and viewpoints expressed by George reflected statements made by Edgar Cayce in his readings "many, many times." I look forward to his providing a definite commentary on George's tests.

But, as I have said, the practicalities of intuitive archaeology will lie in the digging. Unless followed up and demonstrated to be true by the hard proof of excavation, intuitive statements of George and others like him will remain as merely interesting or fascinating stories or theories, difficult to render convincing and meaningful to the scientific archaeological community and to the man on the street. This may be unfortunate, but it is true.

George's readings did provide help and guidance so that a work-able, investigable, and interesting archaeological problem emerged. He stated that on a certain day late in October as the sun sets, the shadow cast by the great Pyramid of Cheops and by the head of the Sphinx overlap, merge, and coincide at a single point on the flat pavement-like plaza area in the direction of the Nile. He suggested that if test excavations were carried out at this point downwards, a chamber containing important records would be found.

There was no mention that this might be the fabled Hall of Records from Atlantean times mentioned in the Cayce readings, but it does exist as a tempting possibility. The recovery of such records would be bound to have a great impact on the world's thinking and upon the spiritual revolution which I have mentioned. At least an excavation plan is quite feasible and should be mounted.

The task of locating the specific merging shadows is not un-complicated, however, because the original height of both the Great Pyramid and the Sphinx must be known to calculate the exact shadow spot. It would seem useful if we could turn the celestial clock backwards in time to a period of more appropriateness from which to determine this exact position. George, however, was able to provide helpful information about the height of the Pyramid capstone and on the dimensions of the Sphinx's original crown. . .now completely missing. This latter height is most crucial to determining the point of the shadow cast. Thus, an interesting problem awaits formulation and investigation; the proof will be in the digging. . .

As I have found before in my intuitive studies, additional relevant information seems to materialize in the least expected places. In this case, it came from two sources: from Mrs. Dorothy Eady, whom we met at Abydos, and from the French psychic Monsieur Raymond Reant, whom George and I went to see in Paris on our return journey.

During our interesting visit to Abydos, Mrs. Eady, an English woman with a fascinating story of her own who had been an Egyptologist of long standing and who was undoubtedly a very intuitive and psychic lady, gave details on the size, form, and dimensions of the missing crown from depictions of the Sphinx and its crown inscribed on stella in excavations around the Sphinx at which she was present.

In Paris we met and consulted with Dr. William Wolokowski of the University of Paris and were introduced to his psychic associate, Monsieur Raymond Reant. Monsieur Reant is an accomplished psychic, and his special field is finding lost persons. He does this by a process of dowsing and clairvoyance, much in the manner of Gerard Croiset. During our evening meeting with Raymond, he mentioned that there was a period in his life when he received a great deal of information on the Sphinx and pyramids; but that since no one would pay attention to him he had thrown the data away. Upon hearing this, I asked if perhaps he and Dr. Wolokowski could seek information on my "shadow problem." I look forward to a report from Dr. Wolokowski and hope it can be incorporated into my Egyptian Research.

The Iranian Phase of the Study

The main objective of the Iranian part of our trip was to determine whether George could intuitively locate the City of the Hills and Plains referred to in the Edgar Cayce readings. Up to this time George had not devoted much of his energies to searching for sites, but I was aware that he could locate them. During an ecological survey by boat in the Parry Sound District in Ontario, when the party was momentarily lost, George, who had never been to the area before, said in an impatient manner, "Keep going that way. It is just around the next point," and it proved to be. It was expected from the readings that the City of Hills and Plains would be located in the Shustar area in Iran.

On October 14, the expedition quickly moved from Cairo through Kuwait to Abadan and Ahwaz, Iran. October 15 was devoted to a visit to the site and Museum of Haft Tape excavated by Dr. E. Negabon, whom we shall meet later on, and to the Zoroastrian ruins of Sese, where the tomb of Daniel is marked by a Ziggarat. After this quick immersion into Iranian archaeological "vibrations," the group settled down at the Shustar Inn, in Shustar, Iran, for four days of archaeological survey.

The travel by jeep was bone-shaking, hot, dry, dusty, nearly waterless, and debilitating. Climbing up and down the high hills and searching the deeply eroded wadis tried the physical resources and health of the entire expedition. Accommodations were makeshift, food strange and new. Several of the members were taken ill, a condition that persisted for the remainder of the trip.

By day two at Shustar, George had successfully located and pinpointed a cave site to the southwest of the town that could well qualify as the cave spoken of in the readings as being associated with the City of the Hills and Plains. However, he did not refer to it in such specific terms. It was well up a deep, eroded wadi.

George said it had been a healing and instruction centre. He said that a grave would be found there and that artifacts of a sur-vival-level technology would be found. He also stated that this site served as a coordinating centre for the activities of caravan trains from distant places. He suggested that there had been an extensive tent city upon the surrounding hilltops.

The absence of evidence of any permanent structures of baked clay, as often seen in Iran, combined with the relative abundance of pot shards littering the adjacent hilltops was mute testimony to the possibility of seasonal trading and the presence of a tent city. This could well be the City of the Hills and Plains if we can accept this definition of a "city."

The area has now been specifically pinpointed and lends itself admirably to an organized excavation. To dig the cave and to test sample segments of the surrounding hills for cultural debris would be a straightforward and manageable archaeological project.

However, this would call for the cooperation and permission of the Iranian government, which currently exercises stringent and effective control over all archaeological work in the country.

George had done an amazingly quick job of finding this site in an area where every set of hills looks like every other set of hills, and where each wadi looks like every other wadi. He seemed to be driven with typical relentless energy to the exact spot. It seemed that the problem of the City of the Hills and Plains was well on its way to solution, but again, the proof is to be found in the digging.

George discovered a second cave site during his third day at Shustar. We drove out eastward to a healing spring which was known to Hugh Lynn and others in the party. Upon arrival at the site, George's intuition again took over. He momentarily observed and studied the spring area, and then he was off up over the rocky cliff surrounding it and into the hills at a furious pace. In fact, we all had trouble keeping up with him, which is not an unusual thing when George is "orienting" himself to landmarks while doing site psychometry.

Before noon of that day, George had pinpointed a cave which is now blocked and obscured by fallen rocks and slides. He located the cave entrance for us by reference to stabilized rock formations in the area. He suggested that this cave, like the first, was a healing and instructional centre and that there were connections between the two. He also stated that the person who had lived and taught there was an early incarnation of Jesus. This was startling information, as was his statement that important tablets would be recovered if the site were excavated.

Despite the rock slides and destruction, George assured us that sufficient portions of the cave remained to merit digging. It would be a much more difficult investigation problem than in the first cave, but a task that should be considered for the proof and the insights it could bring.

At this point, October 19, it seemed that the major objectives of the Egyptian-Iranian expedition had been accomplished and with considerable dispatch. Three positive future excavation programs were capable of formulation. But more was yet to come—for me, the highlight of the program.

We now moved on to Shiraz and visited the great ruins of Persopolis. There George produced an interesting reading. Then to Isfahan, centre of spectacular mosques and bazaars, and on to Teheran. Our main objective now was to meet Dr. Negabon, archaeologist at the University of Teheran, and to visit his field school and research centre. This visit offered us opportunity to carry out a much more controlled study than what had gone on before.

Dr. Negabon's research centre, the Caravansary, was a half-day's drive west of Teheran. The flat plains were dotted with ruins, and we were able to observe an excavation in process. Dr. Negabon was preoccupied with other visiting officials, so our party simply wandered about, observing the excavation and adjacent areas. Our party was hosted to a delightful lunch and I was able to give Dr. Negabon only a brief rundown on intuitive archaeology. He was interested and plans were made to meet him the following day.

Back at the hotel the next afternoon, George recorded an excellent statement about Dr. Negabon's site in the presence of Hugh Lynn, Arch Ogden, Mark Lehner, and me. I was able to put together a summary transcript of that tape and report its contents to Dr. Negabon, who was impressed with the knowledge George had to offer about his site and his comments about it. He was interested in seeing George at work, so several of us met with Dr. Nagabon and Dr. Razee Moazami, our Iranian interpreter, in a quiet room at the Teheran Hilton. Dr. Negabon had a plastic bag full of pot-sherds. These he handed to George without ceremony and said, "George, put them in order."

This George proceeded to do, starting with the oldest specimens and moving through the series of the most recent. As he was ordering the specimens, George also provided comments on the cultures which had produced them. The entire session was tape recorded. One can imagine the impression it had upon the group when Dr. Negabon said, "Your classification is *perfect*, George, I can tell you. . .aside from just a few points. This is significant because you picked them exactly as they came together in the same period."

George's success did not come as a surprise in light of his past performances, but it always is a matter of great relief. To travel to a strange country thousands of miles away, to meet a strange group of ceramics, and to correctly place them in chronological order in a matter of minutes was an astounding achievement and a profound demonstration that the intuitive faculty functions in a mysterious manner far beyond any normal chance probabilities reaching out to produce variable "historical psychic truth."

This experiment appeared to be eminently successful, but the work is not yet done. Both tapes require transcription and close study and scrutiny by Dr. Negabon and myself. I hope that we can perhaps present a joint paper and a considered statement to our archaeological colleagues for interest and assessment.

Toward the end of the session, Dr. Negabon said, "I have a question, George, that is, what was your feeling. . .your very first. . .for a short period when you came to the site?" This question was extremely important because there is a general consensus among researchers in the area of intuition that first impressions tend to be the most important and, hence, most valid. George's highly significant reply is recorded here verbatim, with his permission:

"Ah. . .very old, very old. . .and somewhat sad, too. My immediate impression was that things that I had learned in my country about the Bible and things that they had taught me in Church and things they had taught me about Christianity. . .all of a sudden was not the truth because, I am sorry to say, because I can suddenly see that everything they said in the Bible was just stories that they got from here, you know, were not the truth and I suddenly realized that *this is where it happened*, not in the so-called Holy Land."

A ripple of quiet agreement passed through the hotel room at the Teheran Hilton in response to George's startling statement, but the nodding of heads and the smiles of approval upon cultured Iranian faces seemed to suggest that there was more in what George had just said than met the eye and that perhaps archaeological evidence could well come to light to demonstrate the proposed hypothesis.

As I sat there, I thought of the impact of the discovery of the Dead Sea Scrolls and how that information had set early Christian writings far back into an ancient Near Eastern tradition. It occurred to me that we were faced with a situation where further Christian traditions might be finding themselves set back in a Persian cultural setting.

In summary, it is my assessment that George performed well and with distinction. He completed with success the tasks, however unstructured, that had brought us to Egypt and Iran. We were able to accumulate data to formulate three excavation proposals and had the opportunity to participate in a successful intuitive test case with Dr. Negabon. I consider that it was a highly productive three-week survey, of which this statement will serve as a very, very preliminary report.

Chapter 18

Comments by George

To me the trip to Egypt and Iran was most distressing. If it were not for all the fine people who made up our party there, it would have been a nightmare. I cannot overstate the warmth of Hugh Lynn and his wife Sally, along with Arch and Ann Ogden, Sam and Rufus, the American Egyptologist Mark Lehnar, and his Egyptian wife Suzanne. They were very patient and understanding of the pressure I was under at all times while in the Middle East. It goes without saying that my friends Norm and Ann Emerson and my wife Charlotte suffered, along with every one else, the change in diet and the cultural shock.

To be where all the great prophets had been and to try to recapture new information of the glory of their civilization was a very bold undertaking. There were so many cultures, one on top of the other and intermingled, that the task was mind-boggling, to say the least. I was bombarded with history the moment I stepped off the plane in Cairo.

To try to sort out the "mess," and that is an appropriate word for the pile of human living that confronted me, I asked to be taken to the Cairo Museum first. This visit would help to orient me to the part of history I wished to see. The Cairo Museum is a place like none other. It is a grand building in the middle of a city of some eight million people. The displays inside are breathtaking.

There was so much to see and understand that it would take a person months to absorb it all. There was something from every kingdom of the Pharaohs there. In the Hall of Mummies it was very easy to become ill at the sight of so many dead bodies of ancient people laid out in rows looking very much like they did when alive, although badly shrunken.

Since the trip to Egypt was to be just a warm-up for the later trip to Iran, I was supposed to take it easy. How could a psychic take it easy in Egypt with all that is there to see? It overwhelms the mind just to stand outside the Great Pyramid and look at the colossal structure of the Sphinx; to wonder about the minds and hands that created this. I could see the full beauty of the area at the time they were used. The flowers and other vegetation were as awe-inspiring as the structures. What type of energy force made these flowers, shrubs, and trees grow like this in comparison to the harsh environment that exists there today?

I knew it was different then than it is today. The Nile River flowed just a few yards in front of the Sphinx. The covering on the pyramids was a rosy-coloured, cement-type material from cap to the bottom. There were bathhouses at the entrance in front of the Sphinx and wide steps and terraces leading from the Nile up to it. This is just the minimum of what I saw and why I was overwhelmed.

After a few days in Cairo we went on to Luxor and there we saw the same awe-inspiring type of ruins as were in Cairo. Although they are just piles of stones now, they were unbelievable in their magnificence when they were built.

The trip to Abydos was well worth the bus ride. There is a temple ruin there that still maintains its beauty. The tombs of the pharaohs are in the Valley of the Kings and Queens across the Nile from Luxor. Most people have seen the gold mask from Tut's tomb. The beauty of this is magnified when you see it in place on the statue of the boy king in his tomb.

I can understand Dr. Emerson's frustrations at the way things were uncontrolled as far as a scientific approach was concerned, but I think everyone just wanted to see everything they could and, being intuitive, I saw far more than they did. I should have perhaps communicated what I was seeing to Norm. When we returned to Cairo in the Mena House Hotel near Giza, Norm, Hugh Lynn Cayce, and I sat by the swimming pool. Norm and Hugh Lynn with Turkish coffee, and I with my usual cold beer. I spent over an hour talking about what I had seen, place by place, and except for Hugh Lynn saying, "I heard my Daddy say that many, many times," they listened quietly. After that, I spent another hour answering their questions, and finally they were satisfied.

I can only say that at that time I felt everything was following a path that seemed to be laid out for us as far as my work was concerned. Things were so intertwined with others that it all had to come together to make the whole story. For instance, I could not give a complete story about the ruins in Luxor without seeing the rest of the ruins across the Nile and up the Valley at the Tombs of the Kings and Queens. Even though they were far apart and a river separated them, they were, in fact, just one; and neither was complete without the other.

I knew this was hard to understand, and though I did try to explain it to Norm and he could relate to it, it was impossible for him to see it with my eyes.

We left for Cairo one beautiful morning for our flight to Kuwait. We had to wait at the airport for the plane, and due to the war with Israel there were armed soldiers everywhere. While standing there, my wife Charlotte and Ann noticed a small cat nearby and tried to get its attention. Finally Charlotte asked Mark Lehner's wife Susanne, who is an Egyptian, what to call the cat. She replied, "Try Puss, Puss, Puss," which broke everyone up.

When we finally got on the plane, passengers were, of course, mostly Arabian and these were nearly all men. In this country no one lines up in an orderly fashion to board the plane. They all make a mad dash for it, and God help you if you are in the way. When it was time to board the buses we decided to wait it out rather than take our chances in the wild charge. Hugh Lynn and Sally were unfortunate enough to be caught in the crush. The rest of us waited for the second bus.

My wife and I were seated by an elderly Arab who had the window seat, and though we could not talk we managed with sign language. While sitting there I thought I saw a small puppy dog run past my legs, and I looked at my wife. She thought that she had seen it too, but we ignored it as we thought that it just could not be. When the plane landed, the usual mad rush ensued, with the man beside us climbing over our laps to be the first off the plane.

While we were sitting there waiting to deplane, a woman came down the aisle carrying a basketful of little puppies. We could hardly believe our eyes. We were to learn later that many Arabs try to board the plane with a goat or a sheep over their shoulders. Could you imagine this on our airlines?

When we finally arrived in Iran, it was a beautiful day. The airport was crowded as usual, and there was much confusion before we were on our way. The first day was spent getting to our destination, which was the town of Shustar, and then getting settled. The accommodations and the food was much different from what we were used to. They served mutton and goat meat, and if you did not eat either, as it was in my case, you went without. Many days I made my complete meal out of eggs and eggplant cooked in olive oil. The bread was pita bread, and at breakfast I would cover it with jam and roll it up jellyroll fashion to satisfy my hunger.

We spent the first two days south of the town looking for the city of Edgar Cayce's readings. I did find the cave as mentioned in Norm's text. It was the only thing left after all these centuries, except for the pottery shards which cover the ground.

We went to a healing spring, which I can remember as being ten miles east of the town. The weather was unbearably hot, and, with the sun and improper diet, many people in the group were ill. The spring was at the base of a small cliff. The people from the tiny farm village nearby used it for their water supply.

While we were there cooling off under some trees, a group of girls came from the village and filled goatskins with water. They placed them on their heads to carry them back to their village. The scene was so much like pictures I had seen of Biblical times. This was the way these people still lived. I also saw large piles of Persian melons in the fields waiting for the trucks which would pick them up to transport them to the market. They were delicious to eat, as I found out later.

Above the spring, I could see a small graveyard that served the village nearby. I knew that they never buried their dead, but rather laid them on the ground. They mixed sand and water to make a mud-like plaster with which they covered the body. In the graveyard was a miniature mosque that contained a burial. From the graveyard I could see in the distance another cliff and cave. Even though it was about three miles away over hot dusty sand with the sun shining relentlessly, I knew that it was an important place to go.

I started off not knowing or caring if others followed or not. When I arrived where I had seen the cave, I found that it had fallen in. The scene that I had seen three miles away had been in the past! The cave was a large one, and it had a natural spring coming from the back of it. It had faced to the south, and a large flat plain had been in front of it. I could see a large tent city from hundreds of caravans stopping at the spring for water and shade. Many of the more athletic of our group crawled around the fallen stones and reported that they had indeed fallen in from the roof.

We had a great trip to Shiraz and then on to Persopolis, which was obviously the ruins of a great city; and we marveled at the size of it. Isfahan was most beautiful with its mosques and the bazaars. In Teheran we found a bustling metropolis with a very congested population. The first day there, which happened to be the Shah's birthday, we went to the largest bazaar in Iran. There were parades in the streets and much revelry going on.

The next day, we went about 75 miles west of Teheran to the site that Dr. Negabon was working on. It gave me a chance to look at some very early prehistoric artifacts. It also gave me a chance to assess Dr. Negabon. We then went to his headquarters, or field office, nearby. This turned out to be an old caravansary, which is the equivalent of our modern motel, the difference being that it was built in a square with an open gate in the centre of one wall. In the centre of the square was the courtyard which held a beautiful reflecting pool surrounded by gardens.

The building consisted of several rooms along two walls which opened unto the courtyard. These were the students' quarters. The remaining rooms were taken up with a kitchen, dining room, laboratory, and Dr. Negabon's office. The washrooms were outside. We were served a very delicious lunch which I believe was prepared by the students. They joined us for the meal, seating themselves at a 30-foot table. As few of them could speak English, we were not able to communicate much with them. I noticed that Dr. Negabon ruled his roost with an iron hand.

We did not have a chance to speak with Dr. Negabon, as he had some government officials with him. He did, however, show some interest in my work and suggested that we get together in Teheran the next night. This we did, with good results, as you can see by Dr. Emerson's report. Since Iran has since changed leaders, it makes it impossible to do anything there now. As I have indicated, Dr. Negabon was also a political figure, as one had to be, in order to do anything under the Shah's rule. Therefore it was no surprise to learn that, during the upheaval when the Ayatollah came to power, Dr. Negabon was killed by his students. He was a good archaeologist, and it is Iran's loss.

Now, I must address the end of Dr. Emerson's paper, where I was asked what had first impressed me the most about their country. I had to say the things that I saw that did not coincide with historical thought. I was brought up in the Anglican faith and was from a Christian family, but I never really dwelt on anything to do with the Bible. In Iran I was in the place where Abraham was born and raised, and I saw what he had done and heard the things that he said that are related to him.

I learned that the stories of the Old Testament were the same stories told by his ancestors there in Sumeria. This is where the Garden of Eden had been and where most of the stories of the

Bible had their beginnings. It was here that the first form of writing was invented and the first language was inscribed in clay. The stories were told from one generation to another.

When Abraham went to that part of the world we now know as Judea, he took these stories with him and they were re-told by countless generations. About 900 years before the birth of Christ, they were assembled by the rabbis and written down on papyrus. This became our Old Testament.

I have been to Israel, and it has confirmed my belief that the man Jesus lived as it is said that He did, but not in all the ways it is written in the Bible. I am sorry to say that man has changed and taken out of context many things that were said in those times and misrepresented what really happened. I know I am treading on dangerous ground because, no matter what is said or proven, there are fanatics who will never change even though they may themselves be doubtful at times.

You can see that Dr. Emerson was not as skeptical now as he had been when we started out. He was still puzzled as to where he could put to use the abilities he had at his disposal and with whom he could put them to work. He continued to experiment, tape, and transcribe all he could about our work until he suffered a stroke in 1977, which caused his death in 1978.

Norm kept an open mind and never at any time did I see him lose his patience with anyone with whom he came in contact. On a trip to New Mexico, the people made a mistake and called him "Doc." Norman gave them what he called his "grim" look. To me, this was just a tolerant smile, and it was as grim as I ever saw him look.

I imagine there were times when Dr. Emerson wondered why he was following this course of study, but I realize it was his ever-inquisitive mind that drove him on, despite any obstacles in his path.

The following paper was given in March of 1976 at a symposium at Concordia University in Montreal. It was the last paper he gave before his death. In it, Norm described his work with me to date, much more eloquently than I ever could.

Chapter 19

Intuitive Archaeology: A Pragmatic Study
Dr. Emerson's Last Paper

[This paper was given to a Conference at Concordia University in March of 1976. It was Dr. Emerson's last public statement about his work.]

When I was invited to take part in this conference, it appeared best for me to stress the practical results of my work in what I call "intuitive archaeology." Pragmatic demonstrations are the necessary building blocks of future research and understanding.

For those who are unfamiliar with my work, I will state that my current objective is to seek to bring the disciplines of archaeology and parapsychology closer together to the mutual benefit of each.

The purpose of archaeology is to reconstruct human prehistory as accurately as possible. I have sought to do this by using parapsychological resources.

My task was essentially a clinical one: to seek to assess the truth and accuracy of the information provided to me by my psychic informants. Were they giving me useful and accurate data or relaying imaginative fairy stories? I proceeded with the assumption that such information could be tested against the accumulative knowledge of archaeology, anthropology, and relevant ethnohistorical data.

This study began on January 1, 1971, after I learned that my friend, George McMullen, could "psychometrize." That meant that George could hold an object in his hand, concentrate on it, and almost immediately begin to tell me about it. Presented here is the first reading that George gave me the first time he was given an archaeological artifact for study. I stress that he had never seen such an object before and was not given any information whatsoever about it. I have altered the order of the text to facilitate presentation and my commentary.

George, his wife Charlotte, my wife Ann, and I sat around the kitchen table that Friday morning in George's Peterborough home. George was handed the object without comment, and Ann recorded the event as it took place.

We asked George what the item might be. After long consideration, he replied, "The stem of a pipe" and added that "the larger end is the hot end."

These two statements are correct. It was a pipe stem, and the large end would be adjacent to the pipe bowl and would certainly be the hot end. He then said that they used "a hollow reed in the centre." That was accurate. A study of all the pipe stems at the same site indicated that 98 percent of the holes in the pipe stem had been produced by hollow reeds; two percent had been made by the use of twisted grass fibre.

This was a practice of prehistoric pipe makers. Most pipe stems were made by using hollow reeds, but at one site at least 23 percent of the pipe holes had been made by using twisted grass fibres. The following chart shows the percentage of pipe stem holes manufactured by means of hollow reeds and by twisted grass fibres at six archaeological sites.

SiteName	Number in Sample	% Hollow Reed	% Twisted Fibre
Hardrock	65	100	0
Black Creek	85	98	2
Downsview	82	98	2
Parsons	63	98	2
Payne	54	87	13
Benson	81	77	23

A study of this pipe stem with an illuminated ophthalmoscope did reveal the fact that the hole had been produced by use of such a reed.

Continuing, George behaved like a human holograph machine by describing the whole from the part. He stated, "The part that is missing is much more elaborate than what is here. It took skill to form and make it. The workmanship of the bowl is intricate, smoothly done. . .not terribly intricate though."

George's evaluation that the work was not overly intricate is one which most archaeologists in the area would accept insofar as such pipes revealed an increase in skill and intricacy at a later date.

At that point, George paused to draw a picture of the total pipe that he could "see." We now have a picture of the whole pipe, psychometrically or intuitively derived. We do not have the original pipe bowl for comparison, but we can assess the fact that George's drawing does represent an accurate replica of a past reality that did exist some four centuries ago. *[See Figures 1 and 2 in Chapter 3, pages 29 and 30.]*

We can first eliminate thousands of pipes from all over the world *that it is not.* It certainly is not a modern bulldog, billiard, apple bowl, or bent briar pipe. Nor is it a Plains Indian catlinite calumet, usually called a "peace pipe." Nor is it a Hopewell Culture "moniotor pipe." *(Figure 3.)*

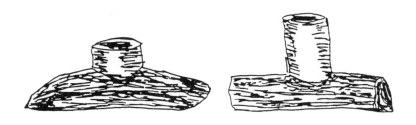

Figure 3. A peace pipe and a moniotor pipe.

Nor is it any of 22 Ontario Iroquois pipe types that I have studied and illustrated. *(Figures 4 and 5.)*

But it is remarkably similar to two Ontario Iroquois pipe types; one is called the Iroquois ring pipe, the other, the Iroquois conical ring pipe. These are distinguished by a slight variation in form only. These two types make up 18 percent—nearly one in five—of the pipes recovered from the site that produced the stem studied by George. There is no doubt in my mind that George was intuitively "seeing" and drawing the actual pipe bowl that he held in his hands. *(Figure 6.)*

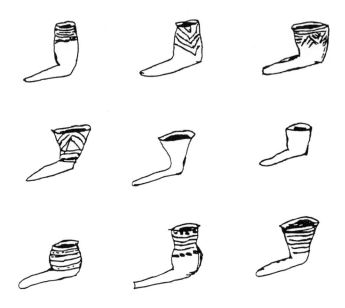

Figure 4. Nine varieties of Iroquois pipes.

George then stated that he could "feel the hands of the maker" and he apparently could also observe those hands at work, for he gave a detailed description of how the pipe was manufactured. He did not specifically state that the pipe was made from malleable clay, but he held his hands over the kitchen table and made a motion indicating that it was made by rolling this way and a hollow reed was placed in the centre. It was made by rolling it conically, small at one end, large at the other, and then it was "bent up." Horizontal line decoration encircled the bowl and "dots were picked in" to complete it.

At this point we have a verbal description accompanied by hand motions, but how can we assess its accuracy? An archaeologist never has and never will dig up an Indian making a pipe. The reports of early traders, missionaries, and explorers are largely silent on the matter. Therefore, we are forced to judge George against the theories and speculation made by archaeologists about pipes. This is done by placing New World pipes in their time and space

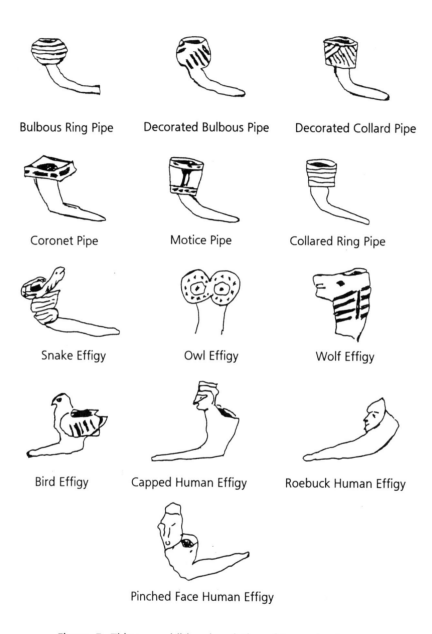

Bulbous Ring Pipe

Decorated Bulbous Pipe

Decorated Collard Pipe

Coronet Pipe

Motice Pipe

Collared Ring Pipe

Snake Effigy

Owl Effigy

Wolf Effigy

Bird Effigy

Capped Human Effigy

Roebuck Human Effigy

Pinched Face Human Effigy

Figure 5. Thirteen additional varieties of Iroquois pipes.

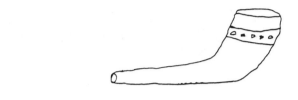

a. Pipe visualized by George.

b. Iroquois conical ring pipe.

c. Iroquois ring pipe.

Figure 6. The projected pipe and real pipe types. Almost one-fifth of the pipes found at the site where the psychometrized stem was recovered were either Iroquois conical ring pipes (5.3%) or Iroquois ring pipes (12.7%).

context and then, by carefully comparing their similarities and differences, educated guesses are made about their origins and development.

The earliest pipes are tubular, linear, cigar-shaped cylinders of clay or stone. The next pipes became expanded or conical in shape, larger at one end but maintaining their linear, horizontal orientation. The next step was to bend up the larger end. Such pipes are often referred to as "obtuse-angled" or "elbow-shaped" pipes. The stem was then distinguished from the bowl.

In the final development, the pipe and bowl met more and more at right angles and the bowl underwent considerable change in shape, size, and decoration. Finally, if we allow the assumption that knowledge of pipe-making was handed down from generation to generation in a gradual and conservative way, we can translate the data into a process of pipemaking which involved a knowledge of ceramic technology and motor habits appropriate to their production.

In the light of reflection, it became evident that what George was describing was a pipe being made in a manner appropriate to the making of pipes relatively late in the series studied.

He was describing, as it were, an event caught and frozen in time: a glimpse of what I call "psychic historical truth." At the same time, he was helping to confirm the speculation of traditional archaeological theory. At this point, it is my conviction that we can credit George with a highly accurate account of the pipe-making process. *(Figure 7)*

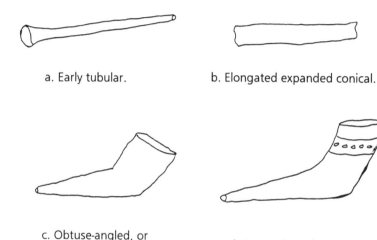

a. Early tubular.

b. Elongated expanded conical.

c. Obtuse-angled, or elbow-shaped, bent up.

d. George's projected pipe.

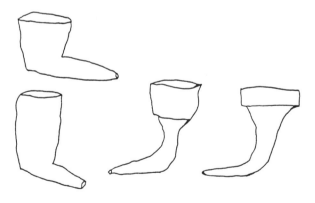

e. Later forms and right-angled types.

Figure 7. Speculation upon the pipe-making process.

George next gave detailed information about the pipe maker who was also the pipe smoker and the person who eventually broke it. He stated, "The owner of the pipe had no teeth. He was 30 to 40 years old. He didn't chew the end of the pipe. He was always tapping it and did this when he broke it. It was broken by tapping it against something."

George continued:

"There was nothing European about these people. The hair was long; the person looks old, the eyebrows heavy, eyes small, heavy lidded, drooped and go around to the corners. The cheek bones were high. . .not Oriental, but high. The lips were thin, flesh lean. . .not dissipated. The person is five foot two, three, four inches. . .not very tall, very lean.

"The person wears a robe or cover for clothing; can't see what the material is. It appears to be black and filthy and dirty with patches.

"The person is unkempt. The hair is tangled; it parts in the middle but it isn't combed. It looks like it grew that way. The forehead is high but not from loss of hair. There were no bags under the eyes; the eyelids were weathered. The rest of the face was smooth, thin, and lean. The ears are prominent and stuck out side ways. The earlobes are small and dark compared to ours. His skin was darker than ours. . .like dark mahogany.

"The person was prominent and well-known among his people because of his age. There were people around him. . .his family around him. What seems odd is that they seem to have a skirt more than pants. The fur side is worn outside rather than inside. It is worn and patchy. There is no elaboration or dressing up or any gay thing about it.

"This is a minimal animal existence, but apparently they didn't use the dress material for their houses. These were brush lean-tos, brush cover for the houses. They were rudely made and not painstakingly. . .material was too scarce."

Such is the very human picture of the old, toothless pipe maker and smoker portrayed by George—scruffy, unkempt, dirty, and bedraggled. Scarcely the noble savage of Rousseau, but he does emerge with some degree of humanity and dignity. . .a person who comes out of the past via psychometric analysis. Is he credible and true? I think so.

Much-needed evidence to check out the detail of George's

chronicles will never be available to us and is lost to traditional methods of archaeological investigation. We have not recovered, nor are we likely to recover, the bedraggled hair.

We will never be able to determine whether this old man lived in a brush lean-to. The village site has been destroyed by the relentless march of civilization and now lies beneath the asphalt parking lot of a pizza palace. But there is a considerable body of knowledge accumulated through archaeology and physical anthropology which will allow us to assess the credibility of George's statements.

There is no doubt that the old man with heavy brow ridges, highly developed cheekbones, and mahogany skin colour is Indian. . .not a white man, not a Negro, and not an Oriental. He is old and toothless, between 30 and 40 years of age. The study of hundreds of excavated prehistoric skeletons have revealed a life expectancy of around 30 years, and a man of 40 would be judged "old." Respect for age is a nearly universal point of view among North American native peoples, and this seems no less true for our old pipe maker.

These people were agricultural—the growers of corn, beans, and squash; and a study of their dental pathology reveals a high incidence of tooth decay, dental caries, and considerable pre-mortem loss of teeth. The occurrence of edentulous mandibles is certainly not uncommon.

The stature of five-feet-two to -four inches is quite consistent with the known range of prehistoric Iroquois males, females being somewhat shorter. It is highly likely that his hair was unkempt and uncombed. No evidence of combs was recovered from the site that produced the pipe stem. Elaborate combs do not appear until much later in the Iroquois sequence. The excavation of the site, although far from complete, did produce evidence of at least one substantial house with walls similar to longhouses of a later date and remains of a quite substantial palisade structure.

Unless it was a very individual thing or a temporary summer dwelling he was seeing, George's statement that they lived in rough lean-tos seems scarcely tenable. However, recent archaeological studies suggest the Huron-Iroquois peoples were subject to periods of harsh, cold weather in late prehistoric times. This could have had a severe effect upon their way of life and be consistent with George's statement that "materials were scarce" and that they lived in a level of "mere animal existence."

George now addressed himself to the problem of locating the site in space. He did this in a matter of minutes. He stated, "Not too far from Toronto. . .I would say within 100 miles. I would hazard a guess the Humber River or the Credit River, or even the East Rouge River. It is not Lake Simcoe, it is not that far east, it is more the Toronto area. It originated within 50 miles or 100 miles of Toronto, on a tributary running toward Lake Ontario, not northward."

George had located the site with uncanny accuracy. He had pinned down and located a very small needle in a very large haystack. Let us put this accomplishment in perspective; it could have been anywhere in the world or any area where I had worked, which could have included sites in Illinois, Wisconsin, Manitoba, the central Arctic, or large areas of northern or southern Ontario—thousands of square miles.

At the time, George knew nothing about where I had worked. Let us say he tuned in to one of 30-odd sites on which I have held excavations in Ontario. I have calculated that this area encompasses about 15,000 square miles. Step by step in his statements, George reduced the area to about 180 square miles, an accuracy of 99.5 percent. To me, it was remarkable.

For those who are familiar with the Toronto area, the pipe stem was dug up at the Black Creek site in the fall of 1948. The ancient village was located on the east bank of Black Creek, a tributary of the Humber River, which flows southward to Lake Ontario. It is just north of the present Crang Plaza on Jane Street near its junction with Wilson Avenue in northwest metropolitan Toronto.

It was an amazing performance by George, and I was impressed. Had I known then what I know now, I would have been more astonished: had I driven him to the area of Jane and Wilson Avenues, he could have led me exactly to where the site had been. I now turn from artifact psychometry to the topic of site psychometry. An opportunity to check out George's ability in this area was provided in the summer of 1973 by the cooperation of the McMaster University archaeologist C.S. "Paddy" Reid.

He was involved in the excavation of the Boyes site near Pickering, Ontario, just east of Toronto. For those unfamiliar with Ontario archaeology, let me point out that the evidence for some structures depends upon the excavation and recovery of what are called "post holes." These are the remains of holes in the ground where posts used in building a structure were once placed. Later, these posts were usually removed and reused for building elsewhere. These holes then become filled with adjacent topsoil, ash and other debris.

Investigating by horizontal excavation will usually produce a series of dark circular soil stains that will contrast clearly and sharply with the normal surrounding yellow-orange sandy subsoil which characterizes Ontario sites. We found evidence of this kind to confirm the intuitive information provided by George at the Boyes site.

When I take him to an archaeological site, George takes a few minutes to orient himself physically to a site and then apparently makes some mysterious shift in his level of consciousness that enables him to see the site the way it was when it was occupied, as if he goes back in time to view it at a point in its physical existence as a village. He can see the houses, people, palisades; even smell the smells, which are not always pleasant.

In this case, our procedure was simple and straightforward. When George could intuitively "see" the site, he showed Paddy where the palisade wall was, including a gateway entrance, and Paddy marked it with metal surveyor's pins. George then walked around the walls of a house that he could "see" (though we could see only the rough, weedy field) and again, Paddy put in surveyor's pins to mark the perimeter.

He then mapped, charted, and recorded this predicted location. These areas were thereafter carefully excavated. Six weeks later, the excavation evidence revealed that George had located these with truly amazing accuracy. *(See Figures 8 and 9.)* The pragmatic results speak for themselves. George can and does provide significant and accurate excavation advice for the archaeologist to test.

Not only did George lead Paddy to successfully locate the structure predicted, but he also provided him with helpful guidelines for future interpretation of his data when he stated that the house to be excavated would be a non-habitation, ceremonial building. Upon being completely excavated, the evidence proved it to be such.

It became clear that the house was not a living structure. It lacked such features as post holes to show the presence of side-wall sleeping platforms. Nor was there any evidence of the storage pits or cooking hearths that are usually encountered. Moreover, the house did show the patterns of a central partition that divided the house longitudinally in half, suggesting the possibility perhaps, of a men's area and a women's area, or some social subdivision which would not be found in the usual living structure.

Finally, Paddy excavated and restored a complete pottery vessel that had been set in the floor of this building. Finding such a whole, restorable pot is most unusual, and I believe that both George and Paddy secretly felt that this was an extra bonus or reward for the faith and cooperation they had shared in each other's work.

To summarize, I quote Paddy Reid at the pragmatic level: "The

Figure 8. Predicted and actual palisade and gateway at the Boyes site. The solid black line marks the palisade line predicted by George McMullen and staked by Paddy Reid. The circular black dots mark the post hole evidence produced upon excavation. The outer outline indicates area excavated.

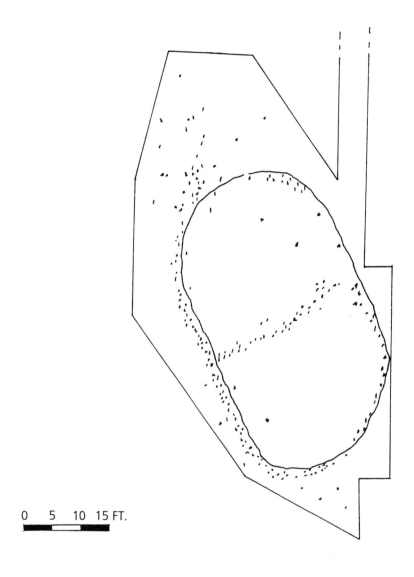

0 5 10 15 FT.

Figure 9. Predicted and actual ceremonial house at the Boyes site. The solid black oval line indicates the house predicted by George McMullen. Black circular dots indicate the excavation evidence. The outer irregular outline indicates area excavated.

implication for excavations where funds, time, and manpower preclude the investigation of an entire site, especially a large village, are thus somewhat staggering, as location of possible structural features prior to excavation would result in major economics of time and excavation efforts."

I certainly agree that major economies in funds, time, and manpower will be achieved by using the psychic resources manifested by George. I would also emphasize his contribution in terms of the depth and richness of the data George provided to the trained archaeologist, which increases our understanding of human prehistory. I hope that the foregoing examples will serve to demonstrate that these psychometric readings do have real pragmatic value that merit further research and serious study of the role of intuition, not only in anthropology but in intuitive living.

Chapter 20

Other Experiences

Excerpts from Dr. Emerson's Papers

[Most of Dr. Emerson's research work was done with me. How-
ever, proof for what I had given him came unexpectedly from others,
and because he was a careful researcher he attempted to explore
as many kinds of psychic abilities and happenings as he could. It
needs to be remembered that in the early 1970s there was nothing
like the amount of information, open interest, belief in, or acceptance
of psychic matters that there is today. Instead, it was surrounded
with fear, superstition, and misunderstanding. People were afraid
that the men in the white coats would come and take you away or
that it was evil—witchcraft. Or the work of the devil.

From Dr. Emerson's papers I have excerpted some incidents
and experiences that he had written about which he termed "mind-
boggling" and that he felt increased and broadened his under-
standing of how this—to him—mysterious ability works. As he came
to understand more, he felt he was able to use my abilities more
effectively. Following are some incidents that did not get included
in his speeches but give insights into what happened and into how
Dr. Emerson thought and felt and how he related them to his re-
search.]

Once I had begun my work with George, seen its validity, and
decided to move into further research with him, it now seems to
me it was inevitable that other psychics would come into my life
and that I would find it advisable to study all the different kinds
of paranormal phenomena to which I had access. As my research
progressed, it brought mind-bending experiences that made it necessary to reassess many of my already-disturbed basic premises and
beliefs.

It can well be imagined that I was rather impressed—not to say
astounded—to learn that when George and I went to visit the ar-

chaeological site of Cahiague at Orillia, Ontario, where I had been conducting digs for some ten years, George told me what follows. He said that when we arrived at the site in the dark of the evening and he opened the gate to allow me to drive my camper-truck in, he was met by no less than six Indian informants who asked him why he had taken so long to get there! Apparently they had been expecting him for a long time.

They went on to explain to George that between the six of them, based upon their combined lifetimes on earth, they possessed a pretty complete knowledge of two centuries of Huron history and prehistory and felt that they could answer "any questions the professor wanted to ask." Astounding, yes, but I assure the reader that these kinds of experiences have become almost commonplace since I initiated my studies with George.

* * * * *

There was an experience in my home where a lady with musical ability and training was "seeing" a ceremony at dawn that the native Indians were celebrating at some time in the distant past and she was able to sing for me (and I recorded) the chant that these people used to greet the sun.

The astonishing thing to me was that George, who was present, was able to see the same event in every detail except one, and this turned out to be merely a matter of terminology or definition.

* * * * *

Although George is full of surprises, he really blew me away one day when he was examining a primitive skull that a physical anthropologist had given him to examine. I was pleased, but not really surprised, when he was able to delineate all sorts of things about it accurately although he had little experience with or knowledge about skulls. What amazed me was that he said that his informants "were no bone experts" and would have to go and find out more information and would bring it back to us in an hour. I could not help but wonder, since physical anthropology is a recent field of specialty, who might be out there for them to consult.

* * * * *

It really opened my eyes wide when a mother brought her young son, whom I had not met, to my house and while there asked him what he could see about me. He reported that there was black around my liver, which meant that there was trouble there. Since two physicians had told me something very similar, I found this most remarkable.

* * * * *

Happenings happen and then what? It is easy for people who do not share an uncanny experience to dismiss it as fantasy, delusion, misrepresentation, or downright fraud. Yet when you are privy to a large number of these, you can no longer explain them away or sweep them under the rug. It is my intention to investigate happenings to the best of my ability and to bring them to the attention of those who are willing to look at them with what I believe is a true scientific method of scrutiny, free from emotionalism, superstition, and prejudice so that they can have the acceptance they deserve to have and find their rightful use in our lives.

As an anthropologist, I know that native people have always accepted such events and abilities as an inborn and useful part of human life and experience. I believe they are natural components of human capabilities; and the sooner we overcome our prejudices and fears and accept them as such, the sooner we can put them to use in a way that will benefit us all.

Chapter 21

Final Comments by George

This was the end of Dr. Emerson's papers on our work together. Since Dr. Emerson's unfortunate death in 1978, many new and innovative things have happened in the field of archaeology. Now it is not so much a matter of an individual archaeologist going into the field alone; there are many other sciences cooperating to help him on his site. There are experts with new tools and understanding about shards, soil, bones, ecology, and geological change. There are electronic Instruments to help add new information.

I hope they will eventually have electronic devices that will do what I am able to do. . .to lay out a site by seeing what is under the ground before digging. There have been great strides made in computers, which can now find and compare artifacts. The advances made daily in the field of computer science affects the work of all the sciences and makes yesterday's work almost obsolete.

I am sure Dr. Emerson would have been a leader in any progress made in innovations to do with his field. Such was his open-mindedness and farsightedness.

With all the new things coming about, I am sure that even my work in this field will be taken over by a more reliable electronic device yet to be invented. But I am sure it will happen, as will some method of finding out how people like me function.

To again quote from Dr. Emerson: "Such is briefly my current understanding of my involvement in intuitive archaeology; pragmatic and potentially useful and researchable, but also mystical and complex."

Dr. Emerson's death was a great loss to those who knew and worked with him. Because of our close friendship and our work together, it was especially hard for me to see our work coming to an end.

The papers presented here cover just some of the highlights of our work. He left countless tapes of our research together; they are in the possession of his wife Ann. It is hoped that eventually they will all be transcribed and published.

As for me, I am still doing the things we started out to do. I make myself available, without charge, to any archaeologists who can use my talents. I have done work for the Mobius Group of Los Angeles. We worked in Egypt and had great success on this project.

Stephan Schwartz of the Mobius Group has written two books in which my work is described. In the book *The Secret Vaults of Time*, he details Dr. Emerson's involvement in my work. *The Alexandria Project* was about my work in Egypt with Stephan's Mobius Group.

I have also done some work in Israel with the A.R.E. and Hugh Lynn Cayce and have worked with others in Canada, the U.S.A., and Mexico, mostly in Yucatan. I have done projects in Australia, Ecuador, and Honduras on the island of Roatan.

As mentioned earlier, in Ontario Dr. Emerson took me to visit a site called Cahiague, which he had excavated for several years. It was the Huron Indian village visited by Champlain. When we arrived, we were met by an Indian named Red Snake, who was our guide through the site. He had been dead for some 400 years. Dr. Emerson could not see him.

Red Snake was later to tell me the story of his life, just before the coming of the white man to our shores. It was intended that Dr. Emerson and I would collaborate on this story. I was to relate to Dr. Emerson what Red Snake said to see if it agreed with historical fact. But the death of my friend Norman left me to write the story myself, which I have done; the book *Red Snake* is now in print [Hampton Roads Publishing Company, Inc., 1993].

I have also written about Red Snake's grandson, Running Bear. That book, soon to be published, covers a later time period and tells of the white man's devastating effect upon the Indians. Additionally, I have written some short stories about Indians and their myths, long past, which were told to me by them at various times and in various places I have visited.

In recent years, I have been working with criminologists Raymond Worring and Whitney Hibbard. This work has taken me to various parts of the United States where different crimes have been committed. We have worked in Montana, Idaho, Washington, and many other states. I have also worked with several law enforcement people in Canada.

During the past ten years, I have worked with an explorer, Abraham Truss of Toronto, Ontario. We have been on expeditions to Australia, Ecuador, Yucatan, Honduras, Belize, France, and many parts of the U.S.A. and Canada. We have traveled to places which even the natives avoid. I have been marooned on an island, up to truck axles in the sand, lost in the jungle, and surrounded by poisonous snakes. We were even lost in downtown Phoenix once and that was really scary.

I still feel that I have a mission to accomplish: to inform people, in this time and space, how people lived, loved and worked in other times and places. History is written by men and they tend to write it from their own points of view. If you are English, history will be written as you see it, but if you are French the view is entirely different. No one has written the native Indian's point of view, and so they have been called heathens and savages. Perhaps if we can see and understand who and what they really were in the days gone past, our perception of them would change, and we could benefit from some of their wisdom.

I have come to know these people from the past, and I can assure you that they felt pain, loved and cared for each other, had dignity, compassion, and intelligence. They had no illegitimate children to put away in orphanages or ship to a strange country as indentured servants. They believed in and prayed to a Supreme Being and were careful to obey His/Her laws.

They had no prisons or poorhouses. They took care of their elderly with respect and love. This is not to say they had no faults, but the Iroquois, for example, did live together in one big house and we could never do that and stay friends for long.

I am afraid that we are influenced by the stories and movies of the Old American West where the cowboys had to fight off those savage Indians. Today, television is perpetuating the same distorted view. I wonder how we or any group such as the English, French, Americans, Mexicans, or other nationalities would feel if we were presented in the same way when we were fighting for our land and our way of life.

It is useless to apologize to my Indian brothers for their treatment in the past. It is better that I try in my space and time here on earth to do what I can to help us to understand their plight and to help where I can. I know from conversations with Dr. Emerson that he felt very deeply for our native peoples, and, though he might not agree with all I have said in the previous paragraphs, he would be sympathetic to them.

In closing, I want to thank Ann Emerson for making Dr. Emerson's papers available to me and for her kind permission to publish them.

About the Author

George McMullen was born in Woodbridge, Ontario, Canada, on January 14, 1920. Seeking to avoid ridicule, he kept his psychic gifts secret from the public until he was in his forties.

In 1969 he began working with J. Norman Emerson, Ph.D., an anthropologist/archaeologist at the University of Toronto. For more than 10 years, from 1969 until Dr. Emerson's death in 1978, the two men did research at various Indian sites in southern Ontario, Ohio, and New York state. Dr. Emerson described McMullen's work in numerous papers delivered to professional groups.

McMullen has traveled extensively in Canada and the United States, as well as to Egypt, Israel, France, England, Mexico, Honduras and Ecuador. He traveled in Egypt and Iran with a group headed by Hugh Lynn Cayce of the Edgar Cayce Foundation, researching Cayce's statements regarding those areas. He also worked in Egypt with the Mobius Group, a research organization based in Los Angeles, California. His work there is prominently featured in explorer/author Stephan Schwarz's two books *The Secret Vaults of Time* and *The Alexandria Project*.

McMullen has done extensive criminological work in several states with Ray Worring and Whitney Hibbard, which the two have mentioned in the books they have co-authored, *Psychic Criminology* and *Forensic Hypnosis*.

Articles about George McMullen have appeared in *Fate*, *MacLean Magazine*, *Canadian Heritage Magazine*, and many others.

He continues to work with archaeologists, criminologists and psychic explorers. He and his wife Charlotte currently live in British Columbia.

His first book, *Red Snake*, captivated readers with its details of the life of a 17th-century Huron. *One White Crow* seeks to shed light on how such a book as *Red Snake* can be authentic. Soon to be published are McMullen's books on the descendents of Red Snake.